BONE-APPETITE!

Homemade Dog Food Cookbook

BOB LOUIS GILLINGTON

Contents

About the Author

A father of four children, Bob Louis Gillington has two children and two furrier children, specifically an adorable Shiba Inu and one ridiculous Husky.

Even with his passion for the outdoors, he managed to work his way up the culinary ladder to become an expert chef, both in the kitchen and in the world of professional culinary arts.

Despite the fact that he is already an expert, he enjoys learning more about his field, and as a dog lover, he determined that the best way to demonstrate his knowledge was to write a cookbook for man's best friend.

Gillington has cooked for numerous critics throughout his life, with individuals instructing him on how to fry, boil, grill, and what ingredients to use and how to use them. The pressure of making sure everything was right, from the raw materials to the end product, took a toll on him physically and mentally.

It wasn't until he started cooking for his pets that he discovered what he had done.

A meal that is made specifically for your furry little pet is virtually impossible to make wrong.

He reasoned that it's better for them in the long run. When you prepare their food, you are aware of the ingredients that are used. He has always cooked for his dogs since they like it so much.

"I prefer knowing exactly what my dogs are eating; there are no colors, cornmeal, or unfamiliar phrases," said Gillington. "They are frequently served chicken or beef stew that they have made themselves. It takes time. We normally cook enough for a week's worth of meals and then start over; it's a never-ending process."

For the purpose of sharing recipes with readers to keep their own furry companions happy and healthy, the author created a recipe book in which the ingredients are readily available to any pet owner.

Gathering sixty healthy homemade dishes for safe pet consumption, this book was made for dog lovers everywhere and anywhere.

ONE

The "Ulti-mutt" Overview!

Dogs, canines, puppies, pooches, hounds, or the most commonly known, *good boy*. Whether your furry companion is a girl or a boy, it's universally accepted to remind them that they are, in fact, a good dog. And like all good dogs, yours deserve all the best in life; this includes their meals.

The dog, as you may know, has been bred from the wolves, their more feral cousins. This means they're largely carnivorous for the most part, but you can't just feed them any meat you find in the freezer or leftovers. Certain meats may not be enough, nutritionally nor physically, for your furry companion.

Most individuals prefer to prepare their own food, including meals for their dogs, and it is believed that this trend will continue in the future. People who aren't interested in the subtleties of nutrition and simply want to prepare a tasty dinner for their dog come through the door when I give nutrition lessons. From the perspective of someone who got into this because their dog was sick, it's fantastic to see individuals with healthy dogs who simply want to do things a little differently now. Their eyes are being opened to the amount of fun it can be, how ethical it is, and how wonderful it makes them feel in the end.

Dogs are group creatures, and when it comes to feeding wild dogs, there is a social procedure involved. The separation occurs when you're sitting at the table and not sharing with your canine companion. Our dogs yearn to be a part of a pack and to benefit from the social connection that comes with eating together as a group.

You can combine a scoop of high-quality kibble with carrots, honey, or a whole egg for a tasty treat. Another option is canned salmon, which is extremely simple and convenient to prepare. If you don't do anything else, try mixing a small amount of canned salmon into your dog's kibble every day. It's one of the most beneficial things you can do for your health.

Other than the fact that grass-fed meat is preferable to organic meat, grass-fed meat is also superior. Given that most luxury dog foods are not genuinely certified organic, it is more cost-effective to purchase organic ingredients and produce homemade dog food instead. In order to avoid eating genetically modified soybeans, which make up the majority of non-organic poultry feed, you should always purchase organic chicken whenever possible.

Some dogs may need more meat; others may just need more protein. Some breeds may need more bone than others, while some just need a softer diet.

Let's take a look at different breeds, see which you have and what you can do about their diet!

Guard Dogs

Starting us off are the fierce and the ever loyal guard dogs. These sweet beasties can start from a manageable 22 kilograms (Appenzeller Sennenhund) to a whopping 100 kilograms (Caucasian Shepherd Dog).

The Usual Suspects

It is widely regarded as one of the best guard dog breeds to own because of its physical strength, protective instincts, courage, and intense family loyalty. If an intruder attempts to enter the premises, a Bullmastiff will almost certainly use his strength to knock them over or prevent them from reaching the exit. The breed, on the other hand, is quite placid in a family setting and makes an excellent companion for young children.

The Doberman Pinscher is a type of dog that originated in Germany in the early twentieth century and is now found worldwide. For those of you with a large piece of property that you want to keep safe, the Dobermann Pinscher makes for an excellent choice for a guard dog for your home or business. This species is incredibly fast, and it is capable of catching up with and dispatching an intruder in a matter of seconds. Breeders of Doberman Pinschers describe them as "courageous, alert, and loyal canines" (Dogtime). Doberman Pinschers are ranked as the world's fifth most intelligent dog breed. As a result, they are best suited to families with large yards and active lifestyles, as they require a great deal of physical activity to maintain.

Cattle guardians by nature, Rottweilers have earned a reputation for being unyielding protectors of their pack when the situation calls for it. In addition to being a highly intelligent breed, they are also loyal to their masters and other members of their family. Rottweilers are known to be reserved when they are first introduced to people outside their family. Aside from that, they are extremely intelligent, making them one of the most effective family guard dogs available.

The Komondor, which has traditionally been used to guard sheep herds, has a natural guard dog ability that comes naturally to him. He is a vigorous, courageous, and loyal breed, and he is well-known for his nobility and fighting prowess on the battlefield. This breed will become a devoted member of the family if it is well-socialized and well-trained from an early age.

Although originally bred for herding, Pulis are extremely intelligent and make excellent watchdogs in their own right. The dogs are constantly on the lookout, and they will bark to alert their owners if they notice anything out of the ordinary. As a result of their exceptional intelligence, they require constant companionship. Given their enjoyment of hiking, running, and other outdoor activities, they are excellent companions for families who lead active lifestyles.

Large, powerful, and dominant canines, Giant Schnauzers are among the most effective guard dogs for homes and families. People who are unfamiliar with them find them frightening, but they are fiercely loyal to their family and friends. It is important to note, however, that this breed requires a great deal of mental and physical stimulation, in addition to constant monitoring and supervision.

As a result of their high intelligence and ability to learn commands quickly, German Shepherds are among the most effective protection dogs available. Because of its boldness, self-assurance, and fearlessness, this breed is particularly popular among police officers. However, when they are with their family, German Shepherds have a calm demeanor, but they will react quickly if their family or home is threatened.

A strong hunting drive and a natural ability to survive in the wilderness are characteristics of this dog breed, which was originally bred to hunt lions and other large predators. Rhodesian Ridgebacks, in addition to being devoted to their owners, make excellent watchdogs. Ridgebacks are known for being selective in their barking, so when one does bark, it is important to pay attention to what is going on around you. It is necessary to teach and handle a Rhodesian Ridgeback in the proper manner in order to prevent him from becoming disobedient. Aside from that, this breed enjoys cuddling and is frequently used as a lapdog for its owners.

Since its introduction into the United States, the Kuvasz has grown in popularity as a home protector. Originally developed to guard livestock, the Kuvasz are fiercely protective of their territory, and they have a strong instinct to protect their family members as well. When in the company of strangers, the Kuvasz is reserved, but he yearns for affection from his family and friends. A constant companionship is essential for this creature because of its high energy levels. It also requires a great deal of physical activity due to its high energy levels.

It is widely believed that the Staffordshire Terrier, which is often confused with the American Pit Bull Terrier, is one of the most effective guard dogs available. Due to the fact that they were originally bred for bear and bullfighting, they have an aggressive and protective nature. This necessitates early socialization and training, which should begin at an early age. Even though they can be intimidating to strangers, Staffordshire Terriers make excellent household pets because they are only known to become aggressive when defending an individual member of the family from harm.

The Shiba Inu is a Japanese hunting dog breed and are classified as small to medium-sized dogs. There are six original and distinct spitz breeds of dogs, all of which are found in Japan. The Shiba Inu is a small, alert, and agile dog that does exceptionally well in mountainous terrain and on hiking trails. Their temperament is not only beneficial for hunting, but it is also beneficial for protecting their human companions.

You may not have noticed, but all of these paw-erful pooches have three things in common: they are all cute, they are all friendly, and they are all adorable. Big and powerful, these pups are full of life.

The best ingredients to put in their bowls are those that will help them bulk up; no one wants to be around an undernourished security dog. Protein, carbohydrates, and a moderate amount of fat should suffice.

To be more specific, you must provide them with a substantial amount of, but not limited to, the following foods: cashews, eggs, fish, peanut butter, and, strangely enough, quinoa.

Additionally, if you have pet birds or cats, either inside or outside your home, these ingredients are excellent choices for them as well!

Lap Dogs

Cuddly, tiny, and absolutely affectionate, you can bet top dollar that the lap dogs' love will certainly keep you warm. Their energy is spent loving you, and their adoration for their family is through the woof! They're so tiny that most people call them toy breeds, but please don't play with them or their heart. No matter the size, all dogs are deserving of a good home and life.

The Love Bugs

Despite the fact that these adorable teddy bears have a lot going for them, it is their upbeat disposition that really sets them apart. Since cuddling is the Bichon Frise's favorite pastime and because they shed little, they are an excellent choice for allergy sufferers and families with young children.

As the Bolognese is affectionately referred to, this small breed thrives in an environment where people are present on a regular basis (hence the name "The Bolo"). So, why would you want to abandon them, is the real question. These gentle companions require only a good brushing every few days in addition to their cuddling.

Besides being perfect for people who prefer to spend their time indoors, these dogs are also intelligent and obedient, and they are easy to train which makes them popular among families and children. The appearance of Havanese puppies is similar to that of stuffed toys, which is due to their double coats.

As a result of their fondness for cuddling with their owners, Tibetan Spaniels are frequently referred to as "comforter dogs." You should not be fooled by their appearances; they are spirited and intelligent creatures who require mental stimulation in order to be completely satisfied.

Is it important to you to have a dog that will provide you with plenty of love while also having a lot of goofy habits? Especially if you enjoy cuddling, Pugs may be the perfect companion for you. To the contrary, this breed is well-known for providing excellent companionship for quiet afternoons spent curled up on the couch with a good book. Keep an eye out for snoring!

They're not only stunningly beautiful, but Cavalier King Charles Spaniels are also incredibly bright and intelligent. Your pet will mimic your behavior, so if you're active, your pet will be as well. If you prefer to relax on the couch, your pet will happily spend the entire day snuggled up in your lap. Breed enthusiasts also claim that they enjoy cuddling with children and other animals.

Have you ever wished you could cuddle up with a big, fluffy plushie that was covered in fur? In a way, the Affenpinscher does come close to fulfilling your dreams. Following your initial acquaintance with him, you will have a lifelong companion and a cuddling buddy.

Their favorite activities include climbing on furniture and licking their paws in a cat-like manner, both of which are displayed by these lovable canines. When it comes to staying healthy, they don't require much exercise, so curl up with a good book, a glass of wine, and a Japanese Chin in your lap and relax.

Even though they have a gloomy appearance, the Brussels Griffon is one of the friendliest dogs you'll ever meet. In fact, because of their ability to completely affix themselves to the humans of their choosing, these dogs are frequently referred to as Velcro dogs by their owners.

Chihuahuas make excellent apartment dogs because they are able to get all of the exercise they require right in their own home. Known as lap potatoes, these cheeky and intelligent creatures enjoy nothing more than cuddling up with their closest friends and family members. They have a tendency to be overly attached to one or two people and may not be able to cope with the demands of living in a household with small children.

Pomeranians are small dogs that weigh less than seven pounds, but they have a lot of personality. You can count on them to cuddle up in your lap whenever you want despite the fact that they are intelligent and active creatures. Grooming a Pom is a lot of fun because it allows you and your pooch to spend more quality time together while doing it.

Pekingese, which have been around for thousands of years and have been beloved by royalty throughout history, are now mostly known as companions and lap dogs, rather than working dogs. With their gentle and loving disposition, you won't have to get up from your couch to spend some quality time with these adorable dogs. Considering the fact that they have a low level of energy, they make excellent therapy dogs.

Breeders of the Chinese Crested dog say that they are well-known for their loyalty, sociability, and playfulness. The fact that they have unusual hairstyles (or lack thereof) makes them stand out in a crowd, but you won't have to look hard to find them because they'll be following your every move, hoping to garner some positive attention.

Since the Shih Tzu has a friendly demeanor and a cheerful appearance, it makes an excellent family pet because it is appealing to both children and adults. Because they're so willing to curl up in your lap, they're perfect for people who spend their days watching television.

French Bulldogs are known for being affectionate and laid-back, and they are the fourth most popular dog breed in the United States. Frenchies make excellent lap dogs because they are a similar size to pugs and, therefore, have a similar temperament. Generally speaking, the French Bulldog is a friendly and quiet dog who gets along well with other dogs and people.

What is the one thing that all of these cuddle bugs have in common? They are energetic, friendly, and diminutive in size.

This means that they don't require large meals, like guard dogs, or anything elaborate, like show dogs, for example. But don't get the impression that you can just throw anything into their food bowls at random; despite their small stature, these feisty little hounds require vitamins and minerals.

Although dogs are primarily carnivores, they can consume certain fruits and vegetables, all of which can provide the nutrients that lap dogs require. Carrots, apples, blueberries, and even honey are all good choices.

Having a rabbit or hamster is also a time saver, as you can go to the grocery store and buy a pack for both your canine and your marsupial at the same time.

Show Dogs

Man's best friend isn't only for security or cuddles! Show dogs like to strut their fluff during competitions and these pretty, precious, polished, picturesque, picky puppies have an extensive and un-expensive diet.

Charming Contenders

Because of their high level of energy and proclivity to follow their masters' instructions, English Cocker Spaniels are considered to be members of the sporty breeds group.

They make excellent show dogs because they have such a positive outlook on life and are always willing to please their handler.

However, their intelligence and vigor make them excellent family pets as well as being well-known for their beautiful hairstyles. Dogs like these make excellent pets because of their trainability and enjoyment of agility competitions.

Speed is a characteristic that Greyhounds are known for, and they can run at top speeds.

Labradors are one of the most popular dog breeds in the world, and their outgoing personalities make them a favorite among dog lovers.

When it comes to speed, Whippets are known for being fast. They are also good competitors in dog contests who enjoy agility exercises and games, just like Greyhound dogs.

Wire Fox Terriers perform exceptionally well in dog competitions due to a combination of intelligence, agility, and responsiveness in their breed. Because of this, the American

Kennel Club has designated this dog as a "master show dog."

Known for their elegant and stylish appearance, Afghan Hounds are also renowned for their long, silky coats that make them stand out among other breeds. These dogs, on the other hand, can be difficult to train because of their strong sense of self-reliance.

Toy Poodles are favored by dog shows because they are intelligent, trainable, and fashionable, among other qualities. These dogs have a demeanor that is similar to that of the Standard Poodle, who is their larger relative.

Bulldogs have become well-known not only as household pets, but also as competitors in dog shows due to their striking appearance.

For the simple reason that these dogs are bred and raised to be hot dogs, it's only fair that their food does not consist solely of hot dogs, don't you think?

Good fats and probiotics are required to keep their award winning coats and agile legs healthy, as well as to keep their stomach bacteria at bay.

Your dogs' coats will benefit from omega-3 supplements, and plain Greek yogurt is a safe choice for keeping their tummies clean. Cats are capable of consuming Omega-3 fatty acids, but I do not believe they are required to consume any yogurt.

Pro Tips!

- Do not feed your dog/s chicken bones. These bones are brittle and small enough that your dog can break it while gnawing on it and the shards may cause internal wounds.
- If you want to feed your dog peanut butter, please check to see if the brand uses xylitol, a sugar substitute poisonous to canines.
- If you have a Chow Chow (a guard dog), please respect its boundaries.

TWO

Ingredients to Fur-get about it

DESPITE THE FACT that your dog isn't picky, as stated in the first chapter, you shouldn't just feed him whatever you want. You're in charge of their health, and they put their trust in you with their lives. If you want your doggy dearest to live long enough to see your children graduate, or if you don't have children, to grow old alongside you, I'll tell you what ingredients you should avoid in this chapter.

Almonds should not be given to dogs to eat for any reason. Almonds can cause esophageal blockage and even tear the windpipe in dogs if they are not chewed thoroughly before swallowing. Water retention in dogs caused by salted almonds is particularly dangerous because it can be fatal in dogs who are predisposed to cardiovascular disease. Salted almonds should be avoided at all costs.

Dogs should never be given the opportunity to consume chocolate. This isn't just a rumor or a piece of folklore, either. Chocolate contains toxic substances known as methylxanthines, which are stimulants that interfere with the proper functioning of a dog's metabolic process. The consumption of even a small amount of chocolate, particularly dark chocolate, can cause diarrhea and vomiting in some pups. If consumed in large quantities, it can cause seizures, irregular heart function, and even death if consumed in large quantities. If you have a dog, you should not keep chocolate in a place where it is easily accessible. As soon as you become aware that your dog has consumed chocolate, contact your veterinarian or the Pet Poison Helpline for immediate assistance. Among the foods that contain methylxanthines are cacao seeds, which are found in the fruit of the plant that is used to make coffee, as well as the nuts of an extract that is used in some sodas. The ingestion of meloxicanthines by pets can result in vomiting and diarrhea in addition to excessive thirst and urination, hyperactivity, abnormal heart rhythm, tremors, seizures, and even death. You should be aware that darker chocolate carries a higher risk of poisoning than lighter chocolate. Chocolate with the least amount of methylxanthines is white chocolate, while the highest concentration is found in baking chocolate.

Cinnamon should not be given to dogs for consumption. However, despite the fact that cinnamon is not toxic to dogs, it is probably best to avoid using it whenever possible. Ingestion of cinnamon and its essential oils may cause dogs to become uncomfortable and ill as a result of irritation of the inside of their mouths. In large quantities, it can cause a dog's blood sugar to drop dangerously low, which can result in diarrhea and vomiting, as well as an increased or decreased heart rate, and even liver disease if consumed excessively. Cinnamon, when inhaled in powder form, can cause difficulty breathing, coughing, and choking in those who are susceptible to its ill effects.

Anything containing garlic should not be given to your dog. In the plant kingdom, garlic is a member of the Allium family of plants, which also includes onions, leeks, and chives. Garlic is five times more toxic to dogs than any of the other members of the Allium family. The consumption of garlic can cause anemia in dogs, which manifests itself in the form of pale gums, an elevated heart rate, weakness, and collapse, among other signs. Garlic and onion poisoning can manifest itself with delayed symptoms, so if you suspect your dog has consumed any of these foods, keep an eye on him or her for a few days rather than just immediately afterward.

Despite the fact that ice cream is a refreshing treat, it contains a lot of sugar, making it unwise to use it as a reward for your canine companion. Some dogs are also susceptible to lactose intolerance, which can be life-threatening. Avoid giving your dog milk entirely by freezing chunks of strawberries, raspberries, apples and pineapples and serving them to him as a sweet, icy treat in place of the liquid.

Because macadamia nuts are toxic to dogs, they should never be given to them as a treat. Aside from nausea and vomiting, macadamia nuts, which are members of the Protaceae family, are known to cause increased body temperature, inability to walk, and lethargy in those who consume them. The worst part is that they are capable of causing damage to the nervous system. Macadamia nuts should never be given to your dog because they are poisonous.

When consumed in large quantities, alcohol-containing beverages and food products can cause vomiting and diarrhea, as well as central nervous system depression and dysfunction, such as difficulty breathing and tremors, abnormal blood acidity, coma, and in some cases, death. Drinking alcohol should be avoided at all costs.

Citrus stems, leaves, peels, fruit, and seeds contain significant amounts of citric acid and essential oils that can cause irritation and, in some cases, central nervous system depression if consumed in large quantities.

If you feed your pet small amounts of coconut and coconut-based products in moderation, it is unlikely that they will suffer serious consequences. Fresh coconuts contain oils that, in some, can cause stomach upset, loose stools, and diarrhea. These symptoms are most commonly seen in the young. In order to prevent this from happening, we recommend that you use caution when feeding these foods to your pets. Coconut water is not recommended for giving to your pet because it contains a high concentration of potassium.

The presence of a toxic substance in grapes and raisins is unknown, but these fruits have been linked to kidney failure in the past. While more information about the toxic substance has been compiled, it is recommended that dogs not be fed grapes or raisins.

Animal products containing bacteria, such as salmonella and E. coli can be harmful to both pets and humans, and these bacteria can be found in raw meat and raw eggs. The enzyme avidin found in raw eggs prevents the absorption of biotin (a B vitamin), resulting in skin and coat problems in animals consuming the enzyme. Consider the fact that feeding your pet raw bones may appear to be a natural and healthy option that would be available if your pet were to live in the wilderness. On the other hand, this can be extremely dangerous for your domestic pet because the animal may choke on the bones or suffer serious injury if the bone splinters and becomes lodged in or punctures your pet's digestive tract.

When pets consume large amounts of salt, they may experience excessive thirst and urination, as well as sodium ion poisoning, which can be fatal. It is possible that your pet consumed an excessive amount of salty foods in one sitting if they exhibit symptoms such as vomiting, diarrhea, depression, tremors, elevated body temperature, seizures, or even death. Due to the high sodium content of salty snacks, such as potato chips, pretzels, and salted popcorn, we strongly advise you to refrain from feeding them to your pets.

Xylitol is a sweetener that can be found in a variety of products, including gum, candy, baked goods, and toothpaste. It is also used to make a variety of medicines. It has the potential to cause an insulin release in the vast majority of species, which can result in liver failure in the most severe circumstances. Hypoglycemia is caused by a rise in insulin levels in the blood (lowered sugar levels). One of the first signs of toxicosis to manifest itself is vomiting, followed by lethargy and loss of coordination. As a result of the signs, it is possible that seizures will occur. In the first few days following the onset of symptoms, elevated liver enzymes and liver failure can be observed in the blood.

While baking with yeast dough, it is possible that the dough will rise and cause gas to build up in your pet's digestive system. The pain that results from this is excruciating, and it can cause the stomach to bloat and possibly twist, potentially resulting in a life-threatening condition. Ethanol is produced as a by-product of the fermentation process, and a dog who consumes raw bread dough may become intoxicated as a result.

Pro Tips!

•White chocolate is less likely to contain the poisonous substance than dark chocolate, so you can give your dog a small piece as a treat. The emphasis is on a teeny-tiny amount. Consider a small piece once every two months for a year.

• Do not give your dog coconut oil, even in small amounts.

• Dogs are permitted to consume yogurt but not ice cream. It is not possible to substitute ice cream for yogurt.

• There is a significant difference between the sodium found in dog food and the sodium found in your pantry; therefore, you cannot use salt to substitute for the sodium found in your dog's dry food.

• It is unlikely that eating a piece of fruit, other than those listed above, will cause any problems other than a mild stomach upset when taken in small doses.

• When it comes to raw meat and eggs, dogs are fine with them as long as the meat has been washed and the eggs come from a reputable source where the chickens have been properly bred.

THREE

The Do and Die-t

Now that the don'ts are out of the way, let's go through the do's. These are ingredients that won't be too "ruff" on your dogs' belly.

Cashews are safe for dogs to eat in small amounts if they are cooked thoroughly. Despite the fact that they contain less fat than other nuts, eating too many of them can lead to weight gain and other fat-related conditions. They are high in calcium, magnesium, antioxidants, and proteins. A handful of cashews is a delectable treat, but only if they are unsalted, as they are when they are roasted.

According to manufacturers, dogs can eat cheese in small to moderate amounts. Cheese is a delectable treat to give to dogs who are not lactose intolerant, which is rare but still possible in some breeds. For those who enjoy dairy products, many varieties are high in fat; therefore, choose lower-fat alternatives, such as cottage cheese or mozzarella. Many dogs enjoy the Himalayan dog chew, which is made of dried cheese; however, we do not recommend that it be shared with other dogs.

Coconut-based products are safe for dogs to ingest, although it is still unsafe to feed them the fresh flesh or milk. Dogs can also benefit from the consumption of coconut milk and coconut oil. This unusual fruit contains lauric acid, which has been shown to be effective in the prevention and treatment of bacteria and virus infections. Bad breath and skin conditions such as hot spots, flea allergies, and itchy skin can also be alleviated with this remedy, which works by clearing the airways.

Can dogs consume corn? Yes, they are permitted to do so. Corn, which is one of the most widely used grains, is a common ingredient in most dog foods and is found in large quantities. Note that corn on the cob is difficult for dogs to digest and may result in an intestinal blockage, so if you are sharing some corn, make sure that it is not on the cob itself.

If the eggs are fully cooked, they are completely safe for dogs to eat and digest. The protein in cooked eggs is a fantastic source of energy, and they can also be used to relieve an upset stomach. It is important to thoroughly cook egg whites before serving them to your pet, as raw egg whites can cause biotin deficiency in some animals.

In terms of omega-3 fatty acids and amino acids, fish is extremely high in both, which are beneficial to your dog's health. Salmon and sardines are both extremely nutritious fish—salmon because of its high vitamin and protein content, and sardines because of their soft, digestible bones, which provide an additional source of calcium—and should be consumed in large quantities. With the exception of sardines, be sure to remove all of the tiny bones from your fish and seafood, which can be time-consuming but is absolutely necessary when preparing fish and seafood dishes. Don't ever feed your dog raw or undercooked fish; only fully cooked and cooled fish should be served to your canine companion. Limit your dog's fish consumption to no more than twice a week, at the very least.

Believe it or not, dogs can consume ham, which is safe but is not the healthiest. A small piece of cooked ham can be shared with them, but it should not be done on a regular basis due to the high sodium and fat content.

The nutrients in honey include a variety of vitamins and minerals, including vitamins A, B, C, D, and E, as well as minerals and antioxidants, such as potassium, calcium, magnesium, copper, and selenium. The feeding of small amounts of honey to dogs has been shown to be beneficial in the treatment of allergies because it introduces small amounts of pollen into their systems, which aids in the development of immunities. When it comes to burns and superficial cuts, honey can also be applied topically to provide pain relief.

Peanut butter is safe for dogs to consume. It is a high-quality source of protein and can be beneficial for dogs. It is high in heart-healthy fats, as well as vitamins B and E, including the B vitamin niacin, which helps the body absorb nutrients. When it comes to peanut butter, raw, unsalted peanut butter is the healthiest option available to you. Before using the peanut butter, make sure it does not contain xylitol, a sugar substitute that can be toxic to dogs. Check the label carefully before using the peanut butter to make sure it does not contain xylitol.

Peanuts, on the other hand, are completely safe for dogs to consume, as opposed to almonds. Healthy fats and proteins can be found in abundance in these. Although peanuts are nutritious, you should only feed them in moderation because you don't want your dog to consume too much fat, which could lead to pancreatic issues. Additionally, avoid feeding them salted peanuts. The digestive system of dogs has difficulty processing large amounts of salt.

It is safe for your dog to consume unsalted, unbuttered, air-popped popcorn when consumed in moderation. In addition to riboflavin and thiamine, which both help to promote eye health and digestion, it contains trace amounts of iron and protein, all of which are beneficial in their own right. If you're giving your dog corn kernels, make sure they're completely popped before you give them to him. Unpopped kernels could pose a choking hazard to him.

Animal protein sources, such as pig's meat, are easily digestible and high in amino acids, and they also contain more calories per pound than any other type of meat. In addition, when compared to other proteins, pork may be less likely to cause an allergic reaction in some pets than other proteins.

Recently, quinoa has begun to appear in some high-quality dry dog foods, which is a positive development. Given its high nutritional profile, quinoa is an excellent alternative to starches, such as corn, wheat, and soy, which are commonly used in the production of kibble. Quinoa is also low in fat and cholesterol.

Your dog can tolerate a few shrimp every now and then as long as they are fully cooked and the shell (as well as the tail, head, and legs) have been completely removed. Succulent shrimp are high in antioxidants, vitamin B-12, and phosphorus, but they are low in fat, calories, and carbohydrate content. Shrimp are a good source of protein as well as delicious.

Dogs can eat tuna, but only in small amounts. If eaten in moderation, cooked, fresh tuna is an excellent source of omega-3 fatty acids, which have been shown to improve heart and eye health. On the other hand, canned tuna contains trace amounts of mercury and sodium, both of which should be avoided in large quantities unless absolutely necessary. As long as no spices are added, the use of canned tuna and tuna juice in small amounts, prepared solely in water and not oil, is permissible as long as no spices are added.

To ensure that your dog is not harmed by eating turkey, remove all excess fat and skin from the meat before serving it. Make sure to keep an eye out for bone fragments because poultry bones can splinter during digestion, causing obstructions or even tears in the intestines in some cases. It is not recommended to feed animals any meat that contains an excessive amount of salt, seasonings, onions, or garlic.

Dogs are capable of consuming wheat and other grains, which is a positive development. Dogs are not required to eat grain-free diets; in fact, it is perfectly acceptable for them to eat grains in moderation. Grains, such as wheat and corn, are excellent sources of protein, essential fatty acids, and dietary fiber, all of which are important nutrients for human health. In the case of a dog who suffers from certain allergies, it may be best to avoid grains altogether; however, this is entirely dependent on the individual dog in question. Consult your veterinarian for guidance on the best course of action.

Plain yogurt is a great snack for dogs because it is low in fat and calories and contains no added sugar. A small number of dogs, on the other hand, may have digestive issues with dairy products. While yogurt is not recommended for dogs who are lactose intolerant, the active bacteria contained within it can aid in the strengthening of the digestive system by providing probiotics. Plain yogurt is the most nutrient-dense of the three options. Avoid any yogurt that has been sweetened with sugar, as well as any yogurt that contains artificial sweeteners, as they are both unhealthy.

Pro Tips!

- Some of these ingredients are best given *below* moderation, others are safe enough to be given in moderation, such as vegetables and pork.
- Make sure anything that can be washed *should* be washed before given to your dog or mixed with other ingredients.

FOUR

Healthy Com-fur-t Food

1 Peanut Butter Balls

PEANUT BUTTER IS a favorite of dogs, and these cookies are an excellent way to sneak some fish oil into your dog's diet. Fish oil improves the appearance and quality of your dog's coat, making it glossier, softer, and healthier.

Organic peanut butter may be found at most supermarket stores these days. Hydrogenated oils and chemicals are included in many commercial types of peanut butter, making them unhealthy. Better still, make your own peanut butter by combining raw peanuts and peanut oil in a food processor and blending the mixture until it is smooth.

Please keep in mind that certain peanut butters contain xylitol, a sugar alternative that is hazardous to dogs even in trace amounts. Check the ingredients list of any peanut butter you purchase to ensure that it does not contain xylitol before purchasing.

Ingredients

- 2 cups of all-purpose flour (white if your dog has allergies)
- 1 cup of rolled oats (or equivalent)
- ⅓ cup of smooth peanut butter
- 1 tablespoon of honey (optional)
- ½ tablespoon Fatty fish oil
- 1 ½ cups of distilled water

Directions

1. Preheat the oven to 350 degrees Fahrenheit (180 degrees Celsius).
2. In a large mixing basin, mix the flour and oats until well combined.
3. Add to a blender and blend in one cup of water until it is completely smooth. The water should be added slowly, until the batter is doughy and thick in consistency.
4. Combine the peanut butter, honey, and fish oil in a large mixing bowl until everything is well-combined and smooth before adding to the doughy mix.
5. Prepare a cooking surface by lightly flouring it. Roll the dough out to make a ¼-inch-thick sheet.
6. Shapes can be created with a cookie cutter. Bake the cookies for 40 minutes on a baking sheet lined with parchment paper.
7. Allow the mixture to cool completely before consuming.

Pro tip: If the dough is too sticky to roll out, gradually add more flour to the dough ball until it is no longer sticky.

2 Chicken Jerky

My Shiba baby gets these chicken jerky treats instead of store-bought rawhides, which he loves. I like that the jerky is rough and chewy because it keeps my dog entertained for a long time. I also like that the chicken contains a high quantity of protein, which is important for a dog's muscle construction.

Ingredients

- 2 to 4 chicken breasts (depending on size).

Directions

1. Preheat the oven to 200 degrees Fahrenheit (180 degrees Celsius).
2. Remove any excess fat from the chicken before cooking it. Turn the chicken breast on its side and slice the chicken breast into ⅛-inch thick strips using a paring knife, turning the chicken breast halfway through.
3. Place the strips on a baking pan and set aside. Bake for 2 hours.
4. Before removing the chicken from the oven, make sure it is cooked through. Rather than being soft or chewy, it should be dry and firm. Before serving, allow the chicken to cool completely on a cooling rack.
5. Refrigerate the jerky in an airtight container for up to two weeks.

Pro tip: If you don't want to use chicken in this recipe, you may substitute sweet potatoes. Sweet potatoes are a nutritious vegetarian alternative to potatoes.

3 Frozen Yogurt Pops

If your dog enjoys chasing ice cubes around the kitchen, he'll go crazy for these frozen snacks. Because they're prepared with human-grade ingredients, including fruit juice and carrots, they provide your pup with an extra vitamin boost. Yogurt contains calcium and protein, and it can aid in the digestion of your dog's meals.

It's important to note that this recipe asks for nonfat yogurt, which is a much better option than other varieties of yogurt, especially if your dog is obese.

Ingredients

- 1 (6 ounce) container low-fat frozen yogurt
- 1 cup 100% fruit juice with no added sugar
- ½ cup carrots, finely grated

Directions

1. In a medium-sized mixing dish, combine the yogurt, fruit juice, and carrots. Stir the ingredients together until they are smooth and well-blended.
2. Drop spoonfuls of the mixture into the ice cube trays to form the cubes.
3. Freeze the ingredients until they are completely firm.
4. Make the sweets in hard plastic trays rather than softer rubber ones, according to the experts. A firm tray makes it easy to take the treats from the tray.

4 Fruit and Vegetable Strips

These strips are a more affordable alternative to the organic chewy treats available at pet supply stores. They are also easily disassembled, allowing you to serve smaller portions as training incentives. Produce high in vitamin C, such as fruits and vegetables, can aid in the strengthening of your dog's immune system.

Ingredients

- 1 tiny sweet potato
- 1 medium banana
- 1 cup grated carrots
- ½ cup organic unsweetened applesauce
- 2 cups whole wheat flour (white if your dog has allergies)
- 1 cup rolled oats
- ⅓ cup water

Directions

1. Cook the sweet potato in the microwave for 8 to 10 minutes, or until the insides are soft and the outsides are crisp. Remove from the heat and set aside to cool.
2. Preheat the oven to 350 degrees Fahrenheit (180 degrees Celsius).
3. In a large mixing bowl, mash the banana and sweet potato until smooth, using a hand masher if necessary. Combine the carrots, flour, and oats in the large mixing bowl. While mixing, slowly add in

the applesauce and water until everything is well-combined.
4. The ingredients will come together to make a soft dough. Roll the dough out on a gently floured board until it is $\frac{1}{8}$-inch thick.
5. Cut the dough into strips using a sharp knife.
6. Place on a baking sheet and bake for 25 minutes.
7. Leftover strips can be kept in the refrigerator for up to two weeks.

Pro tip: Don't be concerned about overcooking the sweet potato. Potatoes that are softer will mash more easily.

5 Beef and Vegetable Balls

Some dogs prefer meaty treats to sweet ones, and this is understandable. These treats have a robust meat flavor and aroma that dogs of all breeds will like. Any time I make these, my dog stands outside the oven door, not particularly patiently waiting for the treats to cool.

Ingredients

- 2 (6 ounce) jars organic beef and vegetable baby food
- 1 cup whole-wheat flour (or white substitute)
- 2 quarts skim milk
- 1 cup purified water

Directions

1. Preheat the oven to 350 degrees Fahrenheit (180 degrees Celsius).
2. In a large mixing bowl, whisk together all of the ingredients.
3. Drop large spoonfuls of the mixture onto a baking sheet.
4. Bake for 12 to 15 minutes, depending on your oven.
5. Allow the sweets to cool completely before serving them. Leftover beef and vegetable balls can be kept in the refrigerator for up to five days.

Pro tip: These treats do not last as long as other types of treats. If you just have one dog, you might want to consider halving the recipe.

6 Turkey and Vegetable Dinner

In this basic dog food recipe, turkey is used for protein, and vegetables are used to provide additional vitamins and minerals. Because turkey contains less fat than beef, this meal is a good choice for dogs who could use a little extra weight loss.

Ingredients

- 4 cups filtered water
- 1 pound ground turkey
- 2 cups brown rice
- 1 cup grated carrots
- 1 cup grated green beans
- 1 tablespoon fish oil (optional)

Directions

1. Cook the ground turkey in a nonstick skillet over medium heat, stirring occasionally, until the meat is thoroughly cooked.
2. Bring a large pot of brown rice, turkey, and water to a boil, stirring occasionally.
3. Reduce the heat to medium-low and continue to cook for another 15 minutes, or until the rice is soft and tender.
4. Add the carrots and green beans and cook for an additional 5 to 10 minutes, or until the vegetables are cooked, depending on their size.
5. Toss with a little salt and set aside to cool.
6. Extra dinners can be kept in the refrigerator for up to five days.

Pro tip: When browning the turkey, avoid using a lot of oil. Because of its high fat content, it may cause gastrointestinal distress in your dog.

7 Chicken Casserole

Chicken, which is a healthy source of protein, and a variety of veggies are combined in this recipe to make a tasty dish. Green beans make your dog feel fuller longer, and veggies help to maintain a healthy intestinal tract for your dog as well.

Ingredients

- 4 boneless skinless chicken breasts
- ½ cup green beans, chopped
- ½ cup carrots, chopped
- ½ cup broccoli, chopped
- ½ cup rolled oats
- ½ cup cooked brown rice
- 4 cups low-salt chicken broth

Directions

1. Using a sharp knife, trim away any excess fat from the chicken breasts and cut the breasts into nickel-size chunks.
2. Cook the chicken breasts in a nonstick skillet over medium heat, turning once, until they are no longer pink in the middle.
3. A large saucepan with the chicken, vegetables, rolled oats, and chicken broth should be able to hold everything. Cook over medium heat until the carrots are soft (about 15 minutes).
4. Toss with a little salt and set aside to cool.
5. Leftover casserole portions can be kept in the refrigerator for up to five days.

6. If you're having difficulties keeping the chicken breasts from sticking to the griddle, a small bit of olive oil can help.

8 Doggy Chili

Dogs require a significant amount of protein to maintain their health and activity levels. The majority of the protein in your dog's diet should come from whole meat sources, such as freshly cooked chicken. Beans are also a good source of protein.

This recipe combines chicken, beans, and vegetables to produce a nutritious and delectable combination.

Ingredients

- 4 boneless skinless chicken breasts
- 1 cup kidney beans, drained
- 1 cup black beans
- 1 ½ cups black beans, drained
- 1 ½ cups chopped carrots
- ½ cup tomato paste (optional)
- 4 quarts of homemade chicken broth

Directions

1. Take away any excess fat from the chicken breasts and cut them into nickel-size pieces with a sharp knife.
2. Cook the chicken breasts in a nonstick skillet over medium-high heat, turning once, until they are no longer pink in the middle.
3. In a large pot, combine the chicken, beans, carrots,

tomato paste, and chicken stock, and cook over medium heat until the chicken is thoroughly heated (about 10 minutes).
4. Allow for cooling time before serving the combination.
5. Chili can be kept refrigerated for up to five days after it has been prepared.

Pro tip: You may boost the omega-3 fatty acids in this recipe by adding ½ tablespoon of fish oil. Even finicky eaters will not be able to tell that there is a healthy element in there because the flavors are so powerful.

9 Beef Stew

This dog-approved version of beef stew is loaded with protein, minerals, and flavor thanks to the addition of vegetables and gravy. As an alternative to commercial wet dog diets, it's a good choice.

Ingredients

- 1 pound ground beef
- 1 tiny sweet potato
- ½ cup carrots, peeled and diced
- ½ cup green beans, diced
- ½ cup all-purpose flour
- ½ cup water
- 1 tablespoon vegetable oil for frying.

Directions

1. Microwave the sweet potato for 5 to 8 minutes, or until it is firm and tender but not mushy. Put it aside.
2. Smaller chunks, about the size of a nickel, should be made from the ground beef.
3. Cook the ground beed in a tablespoon of vegetable oil over medium heat for 10 to 15 minutes, or until the stew pieces are well-done.
4. Remove the meat chunks from the pan and set them aside. Keep the drippings in your possession.
5. Prepare the sweet potato by dicing it.
6. Heat the drippings over a medium-low heat until they are hot. Slowly whisk in the flour and water

mixture into the drippings to make a thick gravy consistency.

7. Stir the pork, sweet potato, carrots, and green beans into the gravy until everything is evenly coated with the sauce.
8. Cook until the carrots are soft, about 15 minutes.
9. Refrigerate until ready to serve.
10. The leftover stew can be kept in the refrigerator for up to five days.

Pro tip: Some health food stores sell readymade gravy, which can save you time and effort in the kitchen.

10 Fruit Parfait

Occasionally, your dog deserves a wonderful dessert to reward him for his efforts. This parfait combines dairy and fruit, so it not only tastes delicious, but it also provides your dog with a healthy amount of vitamins and protein.

Ingredients

- ½ cup plain nonfat yogurt (optional)
- ½ cup strawberries, chopped
- ½ cup blueberries, chopped
- ½ cup homemade applesauce

Directions

1. In a medium-sized mixing bowl, combine all of the ingredients until the yogurt is smooth and the fruit is well-blended.
2. Small portions should be served.
3. Refrigerate for up to seven days.

Pro Tip: On days when you want to serve your pet a fruit parfait, limit the amount of regular food by ½ cup to 1 cup in order to avoid overfeeding.

11 The Old Standard

This was created by Chungah, a self-taught cook who converted her love of cuisine into a successful website and cookbook. Cooking this dinner in huge batches and freezing it as individual meals that can be thawed for days on end is a terrific way to save money.

Ingredients

- 1 ½ cups brown rice
- 2 carrots, shredded
- 1 tablespoon olive oil
- 1 zucchini, shredded
- 3 pounds ground turkey
- ½ cup peas, canned or frozen
- 3 cups baby spinach, chopped

Directions

1. Cook the rice according to package directions in a large saucepan filled with 3 cups water; put aside to cool.
2. In a large stockpot or Dutch oven, heat the olive oil over medium heat until shimmering. Cook until the ground turkey is browned, about 3-5 minutes, stirring constantly, being sure to crumble the turkey as it cooks.
3. Stir in the spinach, carrots, zucchini, peas, and brown rice until the spinach has wilted and the mixture is well heated, about 3 to 5 minutes total time (depending on your stove). Allow for thorough cooling.

12 Scooby's Stew

After her pet became sick, Happy and Yummy creator Michelle had to come up with an inventive way to feed them in order to alleviate their discomfort. Keep in mind that it smells amazing, and if you make it for the first time, your dogs will hound the crock pot and leave puddles of slobber on the floor in front of it while it cooks.

I recommend that you use a strategically placed washable mat to deal with this scenario in order to avoid stepping in a puddle of water.

Ingredients

- ½ cup water
- 1 cup brown rice
- 2 cups cubed sweet potato
- 2 large chicken breasts, chopped into 6 pieces each
- 2 pounds frozen mixed vegetables (peas, green beans carrots)
- 2 cups cooked brown rice

Directions

1. Place all of the ingredients in the slow cooker in the order stated, making sure to completely cover the chicken with veggies.
2. Cook on high for 5 hours or low for 8 hours.
3. Remove the chicken from the slow cooker and shred it before mixing it into the rice and vegetable combination until it is equally distributed.
4. Store in an airtight container in the refrigerator for up to three days, or freeze in single-serve amounts.

Pro tip: Toss some bone broth powder into the stew before serving. It is quite nutritious, and dogs adore the taste. Learn more about the benefits of bone broth.

13 Beef & Veggie Crockpot Creation

Damn Delicious and Chungah's recipes were both included on this list, so it's clear that I'm a fan of their work. The vegetables in this dish can simply be substituted with any vegetables your dog loves (just make sure it's something you know they can eat!).

Ingredients

- 1 pound ground beef
- 1 ½ cups butternut squash, finely diced
- 1 ½ cups brown rice (optional)
- 1 ½ cups carrots, grated
- 1 (15-ounce) can kidney beans, drained and washed
- 1 (15-ounce) can kidney beans
- ½ cup frozen or canned peas
- 4 cups water

Directions

1. In a 6-quart slow cooker, combine the ground beef, brown rice, kidney beans, butternut squash, carrots, peas, and 4 cups of water. Cook on low for 8 hours.
2. Cook on low heat for 5-6 hours or on high heat for 2-3 hours, stirring occasionally, or until vegetables are tender.
3. Allow for thorough cooling.

14 Chicken & Veggie Slow Cooker

From our pals over at the DogBakery, this recipe is paw-fect for smaller, thicker dogs who are lap dogs or dogs who burn a lot of energy!

Ingredients

- 2 boneless skinless chicken thighs and breasts, weighing ½ to 3 lbs each
- 2 cups frozen peas
- 1 big or 2 medium apples, cored and diced (no seeds)
- 1 large or 2 medium sweet potatoes, cubed
- 2 carrots, sliced
- 1 (15 ounce) can kidney beans, drained and washed
- 2 pounds frozen green beans
- 2 tablespoons extra-virgin olive oil

Directions

1. Place the meat in a crockpot and cover with just enough water to cover the chicken breasts. After that, add the potato, carrots, kidney beans, green beans, and apple to the saucepan.
2. Cook on low for 8-9 hours, stirring occasionally. When it is almost cooked, add the frozen peas and cook for an additional 30 minutes on low.
3. When you're finished, drain any remaining liquid and stir in the olive oil until it's mashed (or place in a food processor).
4. Once cooled, portion out daily doses into individual ziploc bags and place them in the freezer. Every

night, take one bag out of the freezer and place it in the refrigerator to thaw for the next day.

15 Turkey & Veggie Mash

Whether you're looking to improve your own health or that of your pet, the Skinny Ms. website is here to help. With all-natural ingredients that are suitable for human consumption, this mash is guaranteed to please your dog. The lean ground turkey and nutrient-dense vegetables are sure to please your pup. We appreciate the inclusion of Safflower oil in this recipe, which helps to enhance the shine of your dog's coat while also providing essential fats for a balanced diet. It's critical to note that when you chat with your veterinarian about preparing your dog's meals at home, you should also inquire about supplements that may be beneficial to them as well as anything else you might supply to ensure that they're getting all of the nutrients they require!

This can vary significantly from dog to dog.

Ingredients

- 2 pounds lean ground turkey
- 1 cup cauliflower florets (cut into small pieces)
- 2 teaspoons raw turkey or chicken liver, coarsely chopped or pureed
- 1 zucchini, sliced
- 2 medium carrots, coarsely chopped
- 1 medium onion, sliced
- 2 tablespoons extra-virgin olive oil
- 1 cup broccoli florets, cut into pieces
- 1 ½ cups water

Directions

1. In a double boiler, bring 1 ½ cups water to a boil. Place the carrots in a steam basket over the kettle and cover.
2. Cook until water is boiling, then decrease heat to a low boil and continue to cook until carrots are starting to get tender, about 10 minutes.
3. In the meantime, place the turkey and liver in a large skillet and sauté over medium-high heat until the turkey is cooked through and the liver is no longer pink.
4. Remove any fat from the pan and set it aside.
5. Simmer until all vegetables are soft but not mushy, 6-8 minutes, depending on the size of your vegetables.
6. Allow vegetables to cool somewhat before chopping them in a food processor or with a knife. The size of the veggies will be determined by the consistency that is desired for the dish.
7. When I make vegetable soup, I normally pulse the ingredients in the food processor about three times to achieve a finely chopped consistency comparable to canned dog chow.
8. Stir in the chopped veggies to the turkey and liver.
9. Toss in the olive oil until everything is well-combined with the turkey and veggie mixture.
10. Allow the mixture to cool before dividing it into freezer-safe portions.

16 Meatballs

While searching for a way to satiate her then eleven-year-old dog Maru, Sumika came up with this recipe. Aside from the meatball styling, this recipe is excellent since it makes use of pumpkin, which is a stool softener and essential for any senior, and oat bran, which helps with a healthy digestive system due to its fiber.

Ingredients

- 10 lbs lean ground beef
- 3 slices white bread, cut into little cubes
- 2 cups oat bran
- 4 quail eggs
- 3 (15 ounce) cans pumpkin puree
- 4 carrots, boiled or steam-steamed, then mashed
- Flour
- 4 kale stalks, neatly chopped

Directions

1. Preheat the oven to 400 degrees Fahrenheit (205 degrees Celsius).
2. In a large mixing basin, combine all of the ingredients, and roll them into balls of whichever size you like.
3. Dredge the balls in the flour, shaking off any excess, until they are lightly coated.
4. Bake until the meatballs are cooked all the way through. The amount of time it takes to bake depends on the size of your balls; mine usually only

take around 25 minutes and are approximately the size of a muscadine or one of those donut holes.

17 Chili

It appears that Shirley, a six-year-old Bernese Mountain Dog, is behind this recipe on BarkPost, which I found to be a lot of fun. The following recipe should only be attempted after extensive research, and it should not be considered a regular meal for your canine companion. However, it is a delicious meal to serve to your dog on occasion, as well as a fun meal to share with your dog because you can easily make a side-by-side version for yourself.

Ingredients

- 1 pound macaroni
- 4 carrots
- 1 (6 ounce) can tomato paste
- 2 tablespoons unsalted butter
- 1 cup beef broth
- 1 pound ground beef
- 1 (8 ounce) can corn (optional)

Directions

1. Preheat the oven to 350 degrees Fahrenheit (180 degrees Celsius).
2. To begin, you must first boil the macaroni.
3. Cook the beef in a frying pan until it is done.
4. Add the butter, carrots, corn, and tomato paste to the beef, and cook for approximately 5 minutes.
5. Transfer your beef mixture to a casserole dish and pour in your beef broth.
6. Bake in the oven for 30 minutes.

18 Meat Cakes

A surprising number of homemade dog food recipes can be found on All Recipes, a well-known human recipe website. In the wake of a food scare for her four dogs, Shelly started looking for ways to cook for them. Even though it's a touch on the rich side for a daily dinner, it's a fantastic treat meal for that special pup in your life every now and then.

Ingredients

- 1 ½ cups brown rice
- 1 pound ground beef
- 3 quarts water
- 8 quail eggs
- 2 medium-sized potatoes, grated
- 4 medium-sized carrots, grated
- ¼ cup extra-virgin olive oil
- 2 large celery stalks, peeled and finely chopped
- 1 ½ cups rolled oats (normal oats)

Directions

1. Preheat the oven to 400 degrees Fahrenheit (205 degrees C).
2. Grease three big 12-cup muffin trays.
3. In a medium saucepan, combine the rice and water until the rice is fully cooked. Bring the mixture to a boil over high heat, uncovered, and simmer for 10 minutes. Reduce the heat to low, cover, and cook for 20 minutes until done. Remove from heat, leave aside for a few minutes to cool, then fluff with a fork and serve immediately.

4. Toss the potatoes, carrots, celery, ground beef, and eggs together in a large mixing dish. Using your hands or a strong spoon, combine the ingredients well.
5. Mix the salt, olive oil, rolled oats, and rice in a large mixing bowl.
6. Fill each muffin cup halfway with some of the meat mixture and press it down to firm it up a little.
7. Bake for 45 minutes, or until the surface feels firm to the touch.
8. Cool for 10 minutes or more on a cooling rack.
9. Turning the muffin tin upside down on a sheet of aluminum foil can help you remove the meat cakes from the pan. To release the cake from each muffin cup, tap the muffin cup on the counter.
10. Refrigerate or freeze in plastic bags that have been tightly sealed.

19 Meatloaf

This recipe is courtesy of Amy Tokic's Pet Guide website, where she reviews pet products, gives advice, and blogs about dog health and insurance. During the fall and winter months, we enjoy eating comfort food, and we know that our dogs will enjoy chowing down on something hearty and nutritious as well.

Ingredients

- 1 pound ground beef
- 12 cups grated mixed vegetables (use the vegetables that your dog enjoys the most)
- 2 quail eggs
- 12 cup cottage cheese (optional)
- 1 ½ cups rolled oats

Directions

1. Preheat the oven to 400 degrees Fahrenheit (205 degrees Celsius).
2. Hand-mix all of the ingredients in a large mixing basin until they are fully blended. In a loaf pan, press the mixture evenly.
3. Bake for 40 minutes.
4. Refrigerate or freeze in slices to make serving easier later on.

20 Dinner Layer Cake

Maggie the Beagle runs the blog Wag the Dog UK, where she shares stories from her travels, tips, and a few recipes. This is the ideal dish to serve at a doggie birthday celebration! Similar to a chicken pot pie but without the crust, you'll find yourself drooling over this dish, too.

Ingredients

- 2 pounds ground chicken
- 1 medium apple, peeled and chopped small
- ½ cup carrots, grated
- 1 quail egg
- ½ cup peas
- 1 cup brown rice (or quinoa)
- ½ cup roasted sweet corn

Directions

1. Preheat the oven to 325 degrees Fahrenheit (170 degrees Celsius).
2. Cook and soften the diced carrots, peas, and sweetcorn in a large pot until they are tender and mash.
3. Cook the brown rice according to the package directions.
4. In a large mixing basin, combine the veggie melee and the rice.
5. Pulverize an egg whole until the shell is completely shattered.
6. In a large mixing bowl, combine the diced apple, egg, and chicken until well combined.

7. Grease or line a cake pan with parchment paper and set aside.
8. Half of the chicken mixture should be placed in the bottom of the cake pan.
9. Place approximately ⅔ of the veggie and rice mixture on top of the chicken base.
10. Place the remaining chicken mixture on top of the vegetable and rice combination.
11. Finish by sprinkling the remaining vegetable mixture on top of the cake.
12. Bake for 35 minutes or until the juices flow clear.
13. Allow to cool before removing from the pan and slicing a piece of upscale chicken nirvana for your canine companion.

21 Crunchy Kibble

The Nest, from the creators of The Knot and The Bump, is a blog that helps new couples navigate their new life and is packed with home, food, and relationship content. This is an excellent first recipe to try if you'd like to dip your toes into the world of cooking at home but don't want to go overboard and would rather progress to the meats and vegetables found in the rest of the featured recipes featured.

Ingredients

- 6 cups flour (you can use white, whole wheat, or oat flour)
- 3 large eggs or 4 medium eggs
- 1 cup powdered milk
- ⅓ cup baking oil
- 2 ½ cups milk, broth, or plain water

Directions

1. Preheat the oven to 350 degrees Fahrenheit (180 degrees Celsius).
2. Prepare a cookie sheet by spraying it lightly with baking spray and setting it aside.
3. In a large mixing bowl, combine the flour and powdered milk with a wooden spoon until they are well combined, then set the bowl aside.
4. In a second mixing bowl, thoroughly combine the eggs, baking oil, and liquid of choice using a wooden spoon.
5. Combine the dry ingredients with the wet ingredients and mix until you have a thick, moist

dough that resembles bread in texture and consistency.

6. In a separate bowl, mix in any additional ingredients you wish to incorporate, such as cheese, shredded meat, pureed fruits, or vegetables. In order to achieve a smooth consistency, add some additional liquid if the dough is too dry. If the dough is too wet, add some flour.

7. Spread the kibble dough onto the greased cookie sheet with a wooden spoon until it is approximately one-half inch thick, then cut into squares. Place the baking sheet in the oven.

8. Bake for approximately 45 minutes, or until it is golden brown and firm to touch. Take the cookie sheet out of the oven and set it aside to cool.

9. Removing the baked "cookie" from the baking sheet and breaking it into bite-sized pieces for your dog is a good idea.

10. Refrigerate the crunchy dog food in an airtight container to prevent it from spoiling.

22 Spinach and Salmon Scramble

This tasty Rachael Ray dish is one you can share with your canine companion, as the meal is also suitable for their human counterparts. Fish oils are extremely beneficial to puppies, but it was surprising how few recipes I could find that included fish as an ingredient.

Ingredients

- 1 teaspoon extra virgin olive oil
- ½ (3 ounce) can skinless, boneless salmon that has been drained
- ½ cup frozen chopped spinach, thawed and drained
- 2 eggs

Directions

1. In a small nonstick skillet, heat the extra virgin olive oil over medium heat until shimmering.
2. Cook until the spinach and salmon are fully wilted, about 3 minutes.
3. Add the eggs and continue to stir continuously until the eggs are cooked through, about 2 minutes.
4. Allow to cool a little before serving in a dog bowl.

23 Vegan Happy Dog Bowl

VegAnnie, a blog managed by Annie, a holistic health coach and PhD student in Austin, provided the inspiration for this stunning recipe. It's certainly not harmful to follow a vegan diet from time to time. Furthermore, with a cost of serving of 64 cents, it will have little impact on your bank account.

Ingredients

- 1 large sweet potato
- 1 (15 ounce) can black beans, drained and rinsed
- ⅔ cup uncooked brown rice
- 1 ⅓ cup water
- 6 kale leafs, broken into 1 inch pieces

Directions

1. Preheat the oven to 400 degrees Fahrenheit (205 degrees Celsius).
2. Pierce the sweet potato with a fork several times around the sweet potato to make it tender.
3. Place on a foil-lined baking sheet and bake for 1 hour.
4. While the sweet potato is baking, prepare the rice in a large stockpot, bring the rice and water to a boil. Reduce the heat to low and cook, covered, for approximately 45 minutes.
5. When the sweet potatoes have cooled, chop them into small pieces.
6. Combine the rice, beans, sweet potatoes, and kale stems in a large mixing bowl and divide into three equal servings.

7. Serve this delectable and nutritious meal to your dog and watch how much they enjoy themselves!

24 Chicken Rice Balls

Raised by three children and a gluten-free diet, Rachelle's gluten-free blog features dishes that she prepares for her family, including several that she has tailored specifically for the family dog Winks. I can't think of anything more satis-fying than a happy ending, but a delicious dog food recipe comes pretty close. These chicken rice balls are delicious and packed with a variety of ingredients that dogs adore, including chicken, sweet potatoes, and eggs. Yum!

Ingredients

- 4-5 cups cooked brown rice
- ½ cup water
- 16 ounces peas, frozen
- 2 whole (4 pound) chickens
- 2 small bunches fresh parsley leaves
- 2 medium orange sweet potatoes (yams), chopped
- 2 small-to-medium bunches kale, stems removed
- 2 small-to-medium bunches spinach
- 8 carrots, peeled and chopped
- 8 eggs

Directions

1. Preheat the oven to 350 degrees Fahrenheit (180 degrees Celsius).
2. Roast the chicken for approximately 1 hour and 25 minutes or until the juices run clear.
3. While the chickens are roasting, prepare the rice (4 cups water and 2 cups rice) and set aside to cool.
4. Peel and chop the yams and carrots, then place

them in a large stockpot with about ½ cup water and bring to a boil.

5. Add in the peas, kale, and apple and mix well. Allow to come to a boil, then reduce heat to low and cook until carrots and yams are tender, about 30 minutes.

6. Transfer the mixture to a food processor with a slotted spoon to remove any excess liquid, then add the fresh parsley and pulse until smooth.

7. Prepare scrambled eggs in their original form.

8. Allow chicken to cool before separating it and adding it to a large stand mixer. On a medium speed, shred the chicken completely.

9. Combine the cooled rice, vegetable puree, and eggs in a large mixing bowl. Scoop out portions of the mixture onto a baking sheet that has been lined with parchment paper. Place portions in a freezer-safe container or baggie after they have been flash frozen.

10. To use, store a day's worth of food in your refrigerator to thaw. I microwaved thawed portions for 22 seconds and frozen portions for approximately 45 seconds each.

11. Feed to your furry child or pet.

25 Woof Loaf

This recipe is courtesy of Popsugar, a well-known lifestyle website. That is not to say that you should be concerned with presentation; after all, yours is for eating, not photographing. Baking loaves is a great way to ensure ease of preparation while stockpiling a large amount of food for the week. Turkey and vegetables, combined with eggs and oats, is a great combination for most canine companions.

Ingredients

- 1 pound lean ground turkey
- $\frac{1}{2}$ cup rolled oats
- $\frac{1}{2}$ cup finely chopped carrots
- 2 quail eggs
- $\frac{1}{2}$ cup peas
- 3 hard boiled eggs

Directions

1. Preheat your oven to 350 degrees Fahrenheit (180 degrees Celsius).
2. Combine the lean ground turkey, chopped carrots, and peas in a large mixing bowl until well combined. Both are beneficial to cats and dogs because they provide them with the nutrition they require for strong eyes and healthy digestion.
3. Combine the oats and eggs in a mixing bowl until the loaf comes together. Oats will make your pet's coat shine, and eggs will provide additional protein. Using olive oil, lightly grease a loaf pan, then spoon half of the mixture into the loaf pan.

4. Make a line down the center of your loaf with three hard-boiled eggs, and cover it with half of the ground turkey mixture.
5. Bake for 45 minutes.
6. Offer your pet a half-inch slice of the cooled loaf, cut from the center of it. He'll be begging for more for sure! If you're giving your cat a slice, it's a good idea to chop it up first before placing it in her feeding dish.

26 Mini Omelettes

Pawsh Magazine is a philosophy website dedicated to appreciating a life well spent in the company of dogs. This healthy recipe is incredibly simple to prepare and takes only a matter of minutes. It is also extremely adaptable—not a fan of green pepper? No problem! Simply swap in a tomato, broccoli, or shaved smoked ham in its place to make a delicious meal. Whatever it is that your little pupster enjoys devouring! The egg provides a wonderful source of protein for your pup; however, make sure that the egg is completely cooked through, as uncooked eggs can cause an upset stomach in dogs. If you cut the dough into smaller pieces after it has cooled, you can make tasty bite-sized treats out of it as well.

Ingredients

- 2 organic eggs
- 1 organic egg white
- 1 green pepper. chopped
- Smoked salmon, thinly sliced

Directions

1. Preheat the oven to 350 degrees Fahrenheit (180 degrees Celsius).
2. Lightly grease an oven-safe ramekin with a small drizzle of olive oil to prevent sticking later.
3. Crack eggs directly into the ramekin.
4. Add pepper and smoked salmon. Stir thoroughly with a fork until everything is well-combined.

5. Bake for 10 to 12 minutes, or until the top is browned and the eggs are cooked through.
6. Allow to cool before serving.

27 Peanut Butter and Bacon Dog Biscuits

From Bill, a father, an animal lover, a successful business-
man, and a self-proclaimed foodie, he enjoys creating new
recipes that are influenced by world cuisine. Do you have a
few slices of leftover bacon from breakfast? This simple
recipe will help you make a tasty treat for your greatest
doggie friend.

Ingredients

- $\frac{1}{2}$ cup oat flour (or rolled oats pulsed in a food
  processor)
- $\frac{1}{4}$ cup smooth, all-natural peanut butter with no
  artificial sweeteners.
- $\frac{1}{4}$ cup finely crumbled crisp bacon, with the fat
  removed
- 1 overripe banana, mashed
- 1 large egg

Directions

1. Preheat your oven to 350 degrees Fahrenheit (180
   degrees Celsius).
2. Fit your mixer with the paddle attachment to
   thoroughly combine the oat flour, banana, peanut
   butter, egg, and crumbled bacon.
3. Roll out the dough mixture to $\frac{1}{3}$ inch.
4. Cut the individual biscuits with a cookie cutter or
   shape them with your hands and place them on a
   baking sheet lined with parchment paper or
   nonstick baking sheet. A small amount of olive oil

can be used to lightly grease your cookie sheet if necessary.

5. Bake for 20-25 minutes or until golden and dry.

28 Beef Jerky for Dogs

From the works of Amanda over at FakeGinger, a DFW food blogger and mother of two sons who calls herself a "mad dog lady."

Ingredients

- Beef that is lean, such as flank, round, or sirloin, should be used. My grocery store sells "thin cut beef for sandwiches," which makes it very simple for me because the meat has already been sliced extremely thin for me!

Directions

1. Preheat the oven to 275 degrees Fahrenheit (140 degrees Celsius).
2. Place a wire rack over a baking sheet with a rim and arrange thinly sliced beef on top of the rack, leaving plenty of space between the pieces.
3. Bake for 2 hours or until the beef is dehydrated.
4. Allow for complete cooling before serving.

Pro tips: Using a wire cooling rack will be necessary for this recipe; therefore, either purchase a cheap cooling rack or use an older cooling rack that you don't care about. I have a special jerky wire rack for this purpose because they just don't taste the same after making jerky. They are definitely still functional, but they do not appear to be the same.

When slicing beef, putting it in the freezer for 5 - 10 minutes will make it much easier to get super thin slices.

This beef jerky should be good for up to a week in the refrigerator. Store it in a ziploc bag (make sure it's one of the thicker ones with a double zipper) and squeeze out as much air as possible before putting it away.

29 Massachusetts' MSCPA-Angell Animal Medical Center Recipe

This recipe is adaptable and easily scaled up. When it comes to the ingredients, you can use whatever you want as long as it's safe for canines. The ingredients in the following recipe are portioned for a 15-pound dog. You can easily adjust the ingredient amounts to correspond to your pup's weight.

Ingredients

- 3 ounces of protein that has been cooked
- 1 ⅓ cups oatmeal, brown rice, sweet potato, and other cooked starch
- 1 tablespoon vegetables
- 1 to 2 tablespoons fat, such as olive oil or vegetable oil

Directions

1. Combine the ingredients and you're done!
2. Before you feed your dog, check to see that the food is completely cool and safe to avoid burns.
3. Experiment with different ingredients to see how it turns out. Maintain the same proportions throughout the meal, and the nutritional value should be retained.

30 Founder's Veterinary Clinic Recipe

Similar to the previous recipe, you can substitute a variety of ingredients with items you already have on hand. For example, you can substitute deboned fish for the main protein source and regular potatoes for the carbohydrate source in this recipe.

For dogs who eat this food, it is recommended that you supplement with calcium or bone meal pattern to ensure that their bones remain strong and healthy.

Ingredients

- ¼ pound skinless chicken breasts, cooked
- 1 cup brown rice, cooked
- 1 tablespoon vegetable oil
- 1 teaspoon salt
- ¼ teaspoon potassium chloride

Directions

1. After the chicken and rice have been allowed to cool, combine all of the ingredients to form a mash.
2. This recipe is intended for a 20-pound dog and is portioned accordingly. You can, however, adjust the amount of ingredients used to suit your needs.

31 VE&CC Vets Healthy Dog Food Recipe

This recipe from VE&CC Vets is straightforward, but it is well-balanced. Ground turkey is the primary source of protein in this dish. The carrots, zucchini, and spinach will be beneficial to your dog's overall health. These fruits and vegetables are not only a good source of essential vitamins and minerals, but they are also high in fiber.

Ingredients

- 1 ½ cups uncooked brown rice
- 1 tablespoon extra-virgin olive oil
- 3 pound ground turkey
- 3 cups baby spinach, finely chopped
- 2 shredded carrots
- 1 shredded zucchini
- ½ cup peas

Directions

1. Cook the brown rice before you prepare the rest of the ingredients to allow it to cool.
2. In a large stockpot, heat the olive oil over medium heat until shimmering. Cook the ground turkey until it crumbled and browned, about 5 minutes.
3. Add the vegetables and rice. Cook for another 3 to 5 minutes while stirring constantly.
4. After the spinach has wilted, remove the pot from the heat and allow it to cool completely before serving it to your canine companion.

32 Zoey's Favorite Fully Balanced Gourmet Dinner

Do you want to spoil your dog and provide them with a meal that they will enjoy? Try out this gourmet recipe for yourself. For the sake of maintaining balance, it contains a variety of different ingredients and flavors that your pup will be begging you to give him more of.

Ingredients

- ¾ cup brown rice
- 1 ¼ cup raw chicken breasts, chopped
- ¼ cup zucchini, finely diced
- ¼ cup broccoli, chopped
- ¼ cup sweet potato, steamed and mashed
- 1 ½ teaspoons extra-virgin olive oil
- Supplement with vitamins and minerals

Directions

1. Cook the brown rice before you can begin preparing the rest of the ingredients.
2. In a large pan, heat the olive oil over medium heat until shimmering. Sauté the chicken.
3. Steam vegetables.
4. Combine ingredients and add supplements.

33 Whole Vet Pet Cooked Dog Food Recipe

This is a delicious home-cooked meal that your dog will devour. The recipe that follows is for a dog that weighs 20 pounds. You can increase or decrease the amount of ingredients to suit your pup's current weight. Supplemental ingredients for nutritional supplements can also be included in the recipe. Cod oil, parsley, and a mineral nut mix are among the ingredients.

Ingredients

- 8 ounces organic ground turkey
- ¼ cup organic vegetables, finely grated
- ½ teaspoon organic coconut oil
- ½ teaspoon fatty salmon oil
- 1 teaspoon raw sunflower seeds, ground
- 500 milligrams calcium citrate
- 2 tablespoons ground turkey organs (hearts, livers, and gizzards)

Directions

1. Blanch the vegetables by briefly boiling them in water. After several minutes in the water, remove veggies and place them in an ice bath to cool. This process softens the fibers while retaining a significant amount of the nutritional value of the vegetable. Once they have cooled completely, transfer them to a blender or food processor and pulse until they are finely ground.
2. Cook the turkey and organ meat gently over

medium-low heat until the turkey is cooked through. Allow the meat to cool completely after it has turned white.

3. Combine all of the ingredients in a large mixing bowl.

34 VetCo Dog Christmas Meal

This recipe from VetCo will help you prepare a festive meal for your dog during the holiday season. It makes extensive use of the leftovers that are likely to be found on your dining room table. Your dog is not at risk from the ingredients. You can whip up this meal in a matter of minutes and spoil your canine companion at the same time. Because the recipe yields a large amount of food, you'll need to portion it out according to the size of your dog.

Ingredients

- 3 pounds turkey meat (cooked, without the skin or bones)
- 1 cup oats that have been cooked
- 1 pound sweet potatoes, cut into cubes
- 2 tablespoons cranberry sauce (with no alcohol)
- 4 tablespoons turkey gravy or olive oil (without onions)

Directions

1. First, prepare the sweet potatoes. Boil them for 20 minutes or roast them for 45 minutes, depending on your preference.
2. Meanwhile, chop the cooked turkey into small bite-size pieces.
3. Cool the sweet potatoes.
4. Combine the potatoes with the oatmeal, cranberry sauce, and turkey meat in a large mixing bowl.
5. Then add your gravy or olive oil to finish it off.

35 DIY Slow Cooker Dog Food

Making a balanced dog meal can be as simple as tossing a few ingredients into a slow cooker and setting the timer for 8 hours. The preparation time for this recipe is several hours, so it's best to complete it overnight or while you're away from home for the day. Alternatively, you can divide the meal into several portions and store them in the freezer for later use.

Ingredients

- 2 ½ to 3 pounds chicken breasts and thighs, skinless and deboned
- 1 medium-sized sweet potato, cubed
- 2 carrots, thinly sliced
- 2 cups of frozen peas, drained
- 1 large cubed apple, core and seeds removed
- 1 (15 ounce) can of kidney beans, drained and rinsed
- 2 tablespoons extra-virgin olive oil

Directions

1. Place the whole chicken pieces in a slow cooker with enough water to cover them and set it aside for several hours. As they cook, they will crumble to pieces.
2. Combine the potato, carrots, apple, and kidney beans in a large mixing bowl.
3. Set your slow cooker to the lowest setting and allow the mixture to cook for 8 or 9 hours.
4. Add the frozen peas at the end of the cooking cycle

and allow the mixture to continue to cook for another 30 minutes on medium heat.

5. Remove the slow cooker pot from the heat and drain any excess water.
6. Stir in the olive oil until it is completely incorporated.
7. Pulse the mixture in a food processor until it is finely ground. You should wait until the meal has cooled completely before feeding it to your dog.

36 Homemade Beef Stew for Dogs

This beef stew recipe will result in a meal that is very similar to the canned options available at your local grocery store. You will, on the other hand, have complete control over the ingredients. The recipe yields enough food for an 11-pound dog, but you can adjust the quantities to suit your needs.

Ingredients

- 1 pound ground beef, seasoned (ground chicken or turkey is also acceptable)
- 1 large sweet potato
- 1 medium carrot, peeled and diced
- ½ cup peas, frozen

Directions

1. In a large pot, cook the beef until it is no longer pink in the middle. Excess fat should not be drained. Due to the fact that it is a good source of fat for your dog, you can leave it in without worry.
2. Throw in the carrots and potatoes. Add water to cover the vegetable and meat mixture, and bring to a boil.
3. Once the water has reached a boil, reduce the heat to low and allow it to simmer for approximately 5 minutes.
4. Add the frozen peas and continue to cook for another 15 minutes.
5. When you're ready to put the food in your dog's dish, wait until it's completely cool.

37 Walkerville Vet Dog Food Recipe

When it comes to the safety and effectiveness of a raw food diet, there is still debate among veterinary professionals. The best of both worlds, according to Walkerville Vet, is recommended. In this recipe, raw food is used to replicate the diet of wolves, which are your dog's natural ancestors. It also takes into consideration the dietary changes that occur in domesticated dogs. It contains raw meat, as well as cooked carbohydrates and vegetables, among other things.

Ingredients

- 9 ounces raw meat
- 1 cup raw carrots, finely chopped
- 1 cup apples, finely diced
- ¼ cup peas, defrosted
- 1 ½ cups pumpkin or squash, finely chopped
- ⅓ cup uncooked brown or basmati rice
- 4 tablespoons sunflower oil
- 4 grams omega-3 fatty acids
- Supplements for nutritional needs

Directions

1. Combine the rice and pumpkin in a pot and cook until the rice is tender. It should yield approximately 3 cups.
2. Allow the ingredients to cool, and combine the remaining ingredients with this mixture, and you're finished!
3. You can freeze this food for up to 2 weeks if you portion it out into individual servings.

38 Chicken Soup

This is a traditional homemade dog food recipe from syd-neywidepetdoors. It's delicious, quick, and inexpensive. Fur-thermore, it will ensure that your dog receives sufficient amounts of essential nutrients. Give small portions of the soup and store the remainder in the refrigerator. You can also store it in small containers in the freezer for later use.

Ingredients

- 1 pound chicken breasts, unseasoned and cooked
- 3 carrots
- 1 celery stalk
- 1 sweet potato
- 1 head broccoli, steamed
- A handful of freshly picked green beans
- ½ cup chicken base water

Directions

1. Cook the chicken in a slow cooker for the best results. Without seasoning, you can prepare it in any way you want.
2. Using a mandolin, slice up the vegetables and place them in a pot. Fill the container with water.
3. Cook the vegetables for 1 hour on medium heat in a large pot on the stovetop.
4. When the chicken is finished cooking, remove the fat from the surface of the broth.
5. Add broth to the veggie pot.
6. Add the chicken to the pot after it has been shredded.

39 Mutt Meatballs

Another banger from sydneywidepetdoors, this homemade dog food recipe will save you both time and money. The mutt meatballs are delicious, nutritious, and simple to prepare for your dog to eat. They can be used as a treat to bring along with you when you go out with your friends. Refrigerate any leftover meatballs in an airtight container after they've been cooked. Because they contain fat, they should not be given to a dog who is suffering from gastrointestinal problems.

Ingredients

- 1 pound lean ground beef.
- ⅔ cup cheddar cheese, grated
- ¼ cup breadcrumbs
- 1 large carrot, peeled and chopped
- 1 egg, lightly whisked
- 4 cups low-sodium tomato paste (optional)

Directions

1. Preheat the oven to 150°F or 200°F.
2. Combine all but tomato paste of the ingredients in a large mixing bowl.
3. Pick out small amounts of meat with a spoon and shape into mini meatballs.
4. Place the meatballs on a cookie sheet and bake for 30 minutes.
5. Heat tomato paste and finish cooking meatballs in the sauce. This step is optional.
6. Allow it to cool completely before serving.

These next eight recipes come from fellow doggy lovers at Petbacker!

40 Vege-rich Turkey Quick and Easy Home Dog Food

Maintain the health and fitness of your dog with this simple, no-fuss homemade recipe—it's less expensive than store-bought and packed with fresh vegetables! It is the ideal supper for your pet because it contains a 50/25/25 ratio of protein to vegetables and grains.

Ingredients

- 1 ½ cups brown rice
- 3 cups water
- 1 tablespoon extra-virgin olive oil
- 3 pounds ground turkey, seasoned
- 3 cups baby spinach, finely chopped
- 2 carrots, peeled and shredded
- 1 zucchini, peeled and shredded
- ½ cup peas, fresh, tinned, or frozen

Directions

1. Cook the rice according to package directions in a large saucepan filled with 3 cups water; put aside to cool.
2. In a large stockpot or Dutch oven, heat the olive oil over medium heat until shimmering. Cook the ground turkey until browned, about 3-5 minutes, stirring constantly, being sure to crumble the turkey as it cooks.
3. Stir in the spinach, carrots, zucchini, peas, and brown rice until the spinach has wilted and the mixture is well heated, about 3 to 5 minutes.
4. Allow for thorough cooling.

41 Delicious Brown Rice and Turkey with Rosemary

This tasty concoction includes the extra smell of rosemary, which will cause your pet to sprint from the other end of your house to get a taste. Made with frozen ingredients plus leftover turkey from supper, this dish is quick and easy to prepare. In addition, it requires only 30 minutes total cooking time!

Ingredients

- 6 quarts water
- 1 pound ground turkey
- 2 cups brown rice
- 1 teaspoon dried rosemary
- 1 pound ground turkey
- ½ (16 ounce) package frozen broccoli, carrots, and cauliflower

Directions

1. Fill a large Dutch oven halfway with water and add the ground turkey, rice, and rosemary.
2. Cook and stir for a few minutes until the turkey is broken up and evenly distributed throughout the mixture.
3. Bring to a boil over high heat, then reduce to a medium heat and simmer for 20 minutes, stirring occasionally.
4. Cook for a further 5 minutes once you've added the frozen vegetables.
5. Remove from the heat and set aside to cool.
6. Refrigerate until ready to use.

42 Easy Crockpot Recipe DIY Dog Food

If your dog is fussy about the food it consumes or has food allergies, this is a beneficial homemade dog food recipe that can be cooked in the crockpot. Simply combine all of the ingredients in a slow cooker and cook on low for a couple of hours. It's time to make some healthy homemade dog chow that your four-legged family member will like! You can also include pulverized egg shells for added calcium and chicken livers for added iron in your recipe.

Ingredients

- 1 (15 ounce) can kidney beans, drained and rinsed
- Frozen butternut squash, cubed
- 1 cup peas, cooked
- 1 cup green beans, steamed
- 1 cup carrots, sliced or diced
- 1 ½ cup uncooked rice
- 4 cups filtered water

Directions

1. Combine all of the ingredients in a slow cooker.
2. Cook, stirring occasionally, on high for 4 hours or low for 6 hours, depending on your preference.

43 Low Carb High Protein Homemade Dog Food

Your pet is a member of the family, and as such, he or she deserves only the finest ingredients, free of fillers, added sweeteners, or spices. Your dog requires protein, which can be obtained through animal meat, seafood, dairy products, and eggs. They require fat, such as that found in meat or oil, as well as carbs, such as those found in grains or vegetables. Aside from that, necessary fatty acids can be obtained via plant oils, egg yolks, oats, and other sources of nutrition The only question is, in what quantities? Following extensive investigation, the author has developed a dish that their dogs adore. This is a must-try!

Ingredients

- 1 cup white rice, cooked
- ½ pound chicken gizzards
- 3 quail eggs
- 2 pounds ground beef
- 14 ounces ground turkey, seasoned
- 6 ounces sweet potato
- 6 ounces peas
- 6 ounces cauliflower or broccoli, chopped
- ½ medium apple, cored and seeded
- 2 cans tuna, in water
- ½ cup cottage cheese
- 3 tablespoons coconut oil (optional)

Directions

1. Cook the rice according to the package directions.
2. In a second pot, boil the chicken gizzards until they

are well cooked, about 10 minutes. Remove from heat. Add the eggs to the pot for the last 5 minutes of cooking time to hard boil them.

3. The ground beef and ground turkey should be cooked until browned in a third extremely big saucepan. Remove the pan from the heat after draining out most of the fat.

4. Using a food processor, grind the raw peas, raw broccoli, raw cauliflower, ½ apple , cooled gizzards, and peeled eggs until they are finely minced and combined. It is possible that two batches will be required.

5. Microwave the sweet potato for 3-4 minutes, or until it is soft and mushy.

6. Using a large saucepan, combine all of the ingredients with the meat and turkey, making sure to include canned tuna. At the very end, stir in the cottage cheese and coconut oil. To incorporate, use a wooden spoon to thoroughly mix the ingredients.

7. This will provide enough food for two nine-pound dogs for two weeks. Place the ingredients in freezer bags and label with the date.

44 Fiber Filled Homemade Dog Food Recipe

If your pet is suffering from constipation, you should give this dish a try. You can also divide it up and freeze it for later use if you choose. Place two meals' worth of homemade dog chow in Ziploc bags and freeze. Take them out to thaw overnight. This recipe will provide you with enough food for around two weeks; however, you should consult your veterinarian to determine how much homemade dog food you should be giving your pet. When it comes time to feed your pet, the author recommends heating the food in a double boiler to ensure that it is well heated.

Ingredients

- 1 pound ground turkey
- 1 pound chicken, shredded
- 1 medium sweet potato, peeled and diced
- 3 cups water
- ½ cup lentils
- ½ cup brown rice
- 2 tablespoons pumpkin puree (not pumpkin pie filling)
- 1 cup spinach, finely chopped
- 2 tablespoons extra virgin olive oil

Directions

1. Cook the turkey and chicken in 3 cups water over medium heat for 20 minutes, or until the turkey and chicken are cooked through.
2. Remove the meat from the water and place it on a plate to cool.

3. Bring the water back to a boil, then add the rice, lentils, and sweet potato, stirring constantly. Cook for 15 minutes at a low heat.
4. Cook until all of the liquid has been absorbed by the remaining ingredients, about 15 minutes.
5. In a separate bowl, combine the cooked meat and serve warm.
6. Keep any leftovers frozen and utilize them as advised by your veterinarian.

45 Homemade Raw Dog Food

For pets that are particularly active, feeding them raw dog food from the freezer department of the pet store will help to improve their energy levels, and their coats will be shinier than ever and their teeth will be in excellent condition. Foods like these, on the other hand, can quickly become prohibitively pricey. A low-cost option that you can produce directly at home is presented here.

Ingredients

- ½ pound ground beef
- 4 ounces chicken livers, cooked
- 1 small apple, cored and peeled
- 1 carrot, diced
- ½ cup baby spinach
- 2 boiled eggs, including shell
- ½ cup plain yogurt
- 1 tablespoon flaxseed meal, ground
- 1 tablespoon extra-virgin olive oil

Directions

1. In a food processor, pulse the carrots, apple, and spinach until they are finely minced but not smooth.
2. Add all of the additional ingredients, except the ground beef, and process until everything is thoroughly mixed.
3. Using a large mixing basin, transfer the mixture and add the ground beef with a spatula or your hands until everything is well-combined.

4. Form the mixture into patties approximately the size of your palm and place on a baking sheet lined with parchment paper.
5. Patties should be frozen until solid before transferring to a storage container or plastic bag and keeping frozen.
6. Remove a day's worth of patties from the freezer the night before and leave them in the refrigerator to thaw before using them for the first time.

46 Homemade Dog Food Recipe for Senior Dogs

Dog food recipes for elderly dogs and those suffering from medical conditions are not as difficult to prepare as they may appear at first. It doesn't even take that much time if you follow the author's suggestions! This recipe was sent to the author by her veterinarian for use in feeding her dog, who is suffering from kidney failure. It is intended to have a low protein content. Consult with your veterinarian before giving food to your pet.

Ingredients

- ¼ pound 80/20 ground beef
- 2 cups white rice, cooked
- 2 cups brown rice, cooked
- 1 hard-boiled egg, peeled and chopped
- 3 slices white bread, crumbled
- 1 teaspoon calcium carbonate (blend a bottle of calcium carbonate until it's a powder, then store in a sealable plastic bag)

Directions

1. Cook the ground beef until it is completely cooked through, about 5 minutes.
2. Combine all of the remaining ingredients in a large mixing bowl.
3. Feed at least twice a day.
4. Don't forget to give your dog vitamin supplements every day.

47 Diabetic Homemade Dog Food

If your dog is suffering from diabetes, this recipe could be a lifeline for him. The author has been making this diabetic dog food recipe for seven years, and she has had it approved by her veterinarian in that time. Due to the fact that the primary component is a lovely yellow bean from India known as chana dal, which has a very low glycemic index (GI), it is a healthy addition to your pet's nutritional regimen.

Ingredients

- 28 quarts water
- 1 (4 pound) bag chana dal, washed and drained
- 2 (1 pound) packages brown lentils, washed
- 2 (1 pound) bags black-eyed peas, washed
- 2 (1 pound) green split peas, washed
- 1 pound pearl barley, washed
- 5 pounds boneless skinless chicken breasts, cubed
- 1 pound ground turkey, seasoned
- 1 (29 ounce) can Libby's pumpkin pie
- 2 (16 ounces) bags frozen broccoli, sliced into pieces
- 2 (16 ounces) bags frozen crinkle carrots
- 2 (16 ounces) bags frozen green beans
- 2 (10 ounces) spinach, chopped and frozen

Directions

1. Fill a 20-quart saucepan halfway with water. Using high heat, bring the mixture to a boil.
2. Combine the Chana dal, brown lentils, black-eyed peas, green split peas, and barley in a large mixing

bowl. Reduce the heat to medium and stir periodically until the sauce is thick.
3. Chicken breast should be cut and added.
4. Toss in the ground turkey.
5. Add in the pumpkin and mix well.
6. Add in the frozen vegetables and mix well. (I cannot fit all of the vegetables in my pot, so I put as much as I can and then thaw the remainder to be added in before storing.)
7. Reduce heat to medium-low and continue to stir regularly until the majority of the water has been absorbed. Allow to stand and cool before putting away.

From Champions to Ice cream, the Breeding Business Cookbook knows what's up with these 10 pawsitively wonderful recipes!

48 Egg Breakfast of Champions

Never fear—a simple, yet stunning Fried Egg, sunny side up, with a little spinach and a side of Doggie Granola Bars is all you need!

Ingredients

- 1 or 2 eggs
- 5 to10 baby spinach leaves
- A sprinkle of dried Kelp, optional

Directions

1. Fry your egg(s) until they are sunny side up.
2. Make a chiffonade out of the spinach, or easily slice them up.
3. Turn off the heat, remove the egg from the pan, and set it aside in the dog's bowl to cool completely.
4. Toss the spinach into the pan while it is still hot but cooling and allow it to wilt for about 15 seconds.
5. Combine the spinach and the egg in a mixing bowl.
6. Scatter some Kelp, an excellent source of vitamins and minerals, on top of the egg.

49 Doggy Granola Bars

It's more of a morning side dish or meal, although it might also be served as a dessert or treat. These treats are quite simple to make, and dogs absolutely adore them. Even the most discerning consumers will be won over by the chicken broth. Yes, there are grains in these bars, but they are healthy grains. Some of the other components, such as toasted wheat germ, whole rolled oats, and quinoa, are quite nutritious as well.

Ingredients

- 2 cups all-purpose flour (rye or whole wheat)
- 1 cup rolled oats (or equivalent, not instant)
- 1 cup germinated wheat
- ½ cup cooked quinoa (or alternative seeds, such as pumpkin seeds)
- 2 tablespoons dry milk powder (optional)
- 1 quail egg
- I cup no-salt or low-sodium chicken broth
- ½ cup distilled water

Direction

1. Preheat the oven to 325 degrees Fahrenheit (165 degrees Celsius).
2. Place all of the dry ingredients in a large mixing basin and mix well.
3. Break the egg into a separate mixing dish and set aside.
4. In a large mixing bowl, combine the water and the chicken broth until well combined.

5. Combine the wet and dry ingredients. Allow for a twenty-minute to half-hour resting period after mixing the ingredients.
6. Measure the size of your baking sheet and cut a large sheet of parchment paper to fit. Using parchment paper is not required; instead, a large cutting board or your counter surface can be used, but I like not to have a sticky mess to clean up later, so I do this on parchment paper and discard it in the trash afterward.
7. Spread flour on the parchment paper and use it to coat the rolling pin.
8. Drop the granola ball onto the work area and begin rolling it out with your hands. You'll want them to be approximately a 12-inch long or a little longer. Depending on your dog's breed and inclination, you can cut them into bars or smaller bits of meat.
9. Before baking them, you can brush on some egg wash to make them a little glossy if you so choose.
10. Cook approximately 45 minutes on a baking sheet that has not been oiled.
11. When making this type of treat or kibble, a secret is to turn off the oven but keep them in there for about 4 or 5 hours to make them a little harder if you like them that way.

50 Chicken, Broccoli, and Rice Dinner

Broccoli is a delicious treat for dogs, whether you serve it to them as a snack or include it in their regular meals. It has the ability to create fresh breath and is high in calcium.

Ingredients

- 5 pounds chicken breasts, diced
- 5 whole eggs
- 5 cups cooked rice (white or brown)
- 3 cups broccoli, finely diced
- 3 tablespoons extra-virgin olive oil

Directions

1. Boil the chicken and rice together until the chicken is almost completely cooked through.
2. Add the broccoli and continue to cook until the chicken is done.
3. Allow the meal to cool before mixing in the eggs and oil.
4. It is also possible to store it in the refrigerator for up to five days.

51 Homemade Apple Crisp Crackers Dog Treats

Aside from the fact that apples are delicious to most dogs, they also include Vitamin C and fiber. Make certain that your dog does not consume apple seeds since they contain a kind of cyanide that is toxic to dogs when consumed in high quantities. Because they are created without preservatives or additives, I prefer to keep all of my homemade goodies in the refrigerator to extend their shelf life and ensure that they are fresh.

Ingredients

- 2 ½ cups whole wheat flour
- ½ cup quick cook oats
- 1 apple
- 1 quail egg
- ⅓ cup coconut oil
- ½ cup water
- 1 tablespoon brown sugar

Directions

1. Preheat the oven to 350 degrees (180 degrees Celsius).
2. Wash the apple thoroughly and grate it, including the peel if desired.
3. In a medium-sized mixing bowl, combine the grated apple, flour, oatmeal, egg, oil, brown sugar, and water until everything is thoroughly incorporated.
4. Lightly dust a work surface with whole wheat flour and roll out the dough to an eighth-inch thickness.

5. Using a knife or pizza cutter, cut the dough into 1 ½-inch x 1 ½-inch squares or 1 x 2-inch rectangles.
6. Using a knife or thin spatula, lift crackers off the baking sheet and set them on a baking sheet that has been sprayed with nonstick spray or covered with aluminum foil.
7. Bake for 20 minutes, then turn off the oven and leave the crackers in the hot oven for another 20-30 minutes, or until the crackers are crispy.
8. Keep apple crisps in an airtight container in the refrigerator once they have been made.

52 Meat-Based Gluten-Free Dog Snack

The ingredients are low-cost, and the end result is a delightful and nutritious dog treat. Lamb and beef are often heavier in fat than other meats. If your dog is overweight, chicken and turkey may be a better option for you.

Ingredients

- 1 pound ground meat (lamb, beef, chicken, turkey)
- 1 large sweet potato, cooked and mashed
- 1 large egg
- ¼ teaspoon garlic powder (not salt) or one large clove crushed into a paste
- 4 tablespoons large flake rolled oats (preferably organic) or ground flaxseed meal.

Directions

1. Preheat the oven to 350 degrees Fahrenheit (180 degrees Celsius).
2. In a large mixing bowl, combine all of the ingredients and thoroughly mix them together.
3. Lightly coat a cookie sheet with olive oil to prevent sticking.
4. Pour the ingredients onto a cookie sheet and spread them out evenly and flatly to the edges of the baking sheet. This should be between a quarter and a half inch thick.
5. Bake for 1 hour for best results.
6. Remove the pan from the oven and, if you choose, cut out shapes with your cookie cutter. If you don't have a cookie cutter, you may simply cut the cookie

dough into squares using a knife or a pizza cutter if you don't have one.

7. Cook for another hour at 250 degrees Fahrenheit. This will cause the nutritious dog treats to become dried out. Keep an eye on the temperature of your oven. Depending on how hot your oven operates, the duration may be extended or shortened. These dog cookies should be quite dry and a touch crispy on the outside, but not burned on the inside.

8. Remove from the oven and cool.

53 Sweet Potato Dog Chew Treats

A sweet for your sweetie!

Ingredients

- Large sweet potatoes

Directions

1. Preheat the oven to the lowest temperature.
2. While the oven is preheating, chop one top off each sweet potato to make it easier to balance when slicing. Cut thick lengthwise slices of the sweet potato with a sharp knife or a mandoline, about 1/3 inch thick for larger chews, and carefully place them on a baking sheet. Trust me when I say that you want them thick because after they are dehydrated, the slices will lose the majority of their thickness.
3. Prepare baking sheets by greasing them and arranging slices on the level surface of the pans. Place the pans on the uppermost racks of the oven and allow them to do their thing...for a long time!
4. We cooked and dehydrated ours slowly over a period of approximately 8 hours, give or take a few minutes. The higher the heat setting, the less time you will need; but, the lower the setting and the longer the period, the better the overall result will be.

54 Pumpkin Spice Puppuccinos

Because pumpkin-everything is currently in full swing, I thought I'd provide a unique dish for our four-legged pals.

Ingredients

- ¼ cup coconut milk, unsweetened (almond milk or goat milk)
- ¼ teaspoon freshly ground cinnamon
- 1 cup pure pumpkin

Directions

1. Blend all of the ingredients together in a blender.
2. Blend until everything is well combined.
3. Pour into tiny serving cups and set aside (or freeze using ice cube trays).
4. If you like a thinner consistency, add an additional dash of coconut milk.

55 Pup-R-Mints Homemade Breath Freshening Dog Treats

In addition to being beneficial to the skin, coconut oil has been shown to help reduce bad dog breath.

Ingredients

- 1 cup whole wheat flour
- 1 egg
- 6 to 8 sprigs parsley
- 6 to 8 mint sprigs
- ⅓ cup plain yogurt
- ½ cup beef broth
- 3 tablespoons coconut oil
- 2 to 3 drops peppermint essential oil

Directions

1. Preheat the oven to 350 degrees Fahrenheit (180 degrees Celsius).
2. Puree the coconut oil with the parsley and mint in a food processor, a chopper, or a blender until the herbs are finely chopped.
3. In a separate dish, whisk together the yogurt, egg, and broth until well combined.
4. Add a drop or two of peppermint extract to the mixture to enhance the mint flavor.
5. Combine flour, coconut oil, and herbs in a large mixing bowl.
6. Using your hands, blend the ingredients until they are thoroughly incorporated.

7. Form the dough into ping pong-sized balls with your hands. Make a flat press using your fingers.
8. Cooking spray or parchment paper should be used to line a baking sheet.
9. Arrange cookies on a baking sheet 1-inch apart.
10. Continue to cook for 10-12 minutes, or until the edges begin to become golden brown.

56 Bacon and Cheddar Mutt-fins

It's the perfect breakfast treat or anytime you want to offer your dog a little extra affection.

Ingredients

- 1 cup whole wheat flour
- 2 slices bacon, cooked
- 1 cup cheddar cheese, shredded
- 2 tablespoons vegetable oil
- 2 teaspoons baking powder
- 2 tablespoons ground flaxseed
- ½ cup unsweetened condensed milk
- 2 large eggs

Directions

1. Preheat the oven to 350 degrees Fahrenheit (180 degrees Celsius).
2. Finely chop the bacon into small pieces.
3. In a medium bowl, add all of the ingredients and stir until everything is well-combined.
4. Spray a nonstick spray into a muffin tray and set aside.
5. Using a measuring spoon, scoop approximately 1 tablespoon of batter into each muffin cup and set aside.
6. Bake for 20-25 minutes, or until the tops are lightly browned on the edges.
7. Allow to cool completely before using.
8. Store in an airtight container in the refrigerator for

7-10 days or in the freezer for up to 2 months after preparation.

57 Soup for Dogs

Broths are beneficial for a wide variety of dogs. They are particularly useful when your pet's appetite is poor, when the weather is warm, or when you need to feed your pet only sparingly for a couple of days. Pets who are overweight can benefit from them as meal substitutes as part of a weight-loss program, and they can also be used to support modified fasting practices. Here are a few recipes for you to experiment with.

Ingredients

- 25 ounces raw, lean lamb
- 2 litres water
- Carrots, grated or diced
- 1 cup oats
- ¼ cup pearl barley
- 1 tablespoon parsley, chopped

Directions

1. Prepare the meat by chopping it up and placing it in a pan. Cover the meat with water and bring the pot to a boil.
2. After the first 90 minutes, add the barley and carrot and continue to cook for another 60 minutes.
3. Toward the end of the cooking process, sprinkle with the parsley.
4. Allow it cool completely before removing any excess fat.
5. Divide the mixture into multiple meals over the course of one to two days.

58 Easy Three-ingredient Dog Ice Cream

Help your favorite four-legged buddy get through the dog days of summer's sweltering temperatures!

Ingredients

- 1 (32 ounce) container plain yogurt
- ½ cup pure coconut butter
- 1 cup fresh strawberries, cleaned and dried
- 1 cup dried strawberries

Directions

1. In a blender, combine the yogurt, strawberries, and coconut butter, and blend until completely smooth.
2. Pour the mixture into a container that can be frozen. Pour the mixture into ice cube trays or tiny food-safe containers to create individual servings.
3. Cover with plastic wrap and place in the freezer for several hours or up to a day before serving.
4. Scoop single portions into your dog's favorite bowl after they have been frozen. Leftovers should be kept in the freezer. This recipe yields around 5 cups.

Our final two recipes are from the lovely Wendy Nan Reese form The Natural Pet Food Cookbook!

59 Ham Upside-Down Casserole

My boys adore ham, so I utilize leftovers to create this tasty meal, and I usually have some on hand in the freezer for emergencies. When stored in an airtight container, this dish will keep for four days in the refrigerator and three months in the freezer.

Ingredients

- 1 ½ cups cubed ham, cooked
- 1 cup lima beans, cooked and drained
- 1 (8 ounce) can cream-style corn
- 1 cup of oats
- 4 ounces cheddar cheese, shredded
- 1 tablespoon Worcestershire sauce
- ¼ cup fresh parsley, finely chopped (1 ⅓ tablespoons parsley flakes)
- 2 teaspoons butter, melted
- ⅓ cup flour
- ⅓ cup cornmeal
- 2 tablespoons unbleached wheat germ
- 1 egg
- ¼ cup of milk
- Fresh parsley for garnish

Directions

1. Preheat the oven to 400 degrees Fahrenheit (205 degrees Celsius).
2. Spray 8-inch casserole dish with nonstick cooking spray.
3. Combine the ham, lima beans, corn, cheese,

Worcestershire sauce, and parsley in a large mixing basin until well combined.

4. Pour the mixture into the prepared casserole dish, cover with aluminum foil, and bake for 15 minutes.
5. The other ingredients should be mixed together in a smaller mixing dish.
6. Pour the batter over the hot meat mixture, spreading it evenly to the sides of the pan.
7. Bake for 20 minutes, or until the top is golden brown and the potatoes are cooked through. It should be possible to insert a knife into the middle and have it come out clean. Allow it cool completely before cutting into wedges and inverting each wedge onto a plate.
8. If you have some fresh parsley on hand, use it as a garnish for this dish.

60 Nautical Navy Bean Soup

Despite the fact that I never allow my dogs to consume the ham bone, if I'm going to freeze the soup (or even chill it), I always keep it with the ham bone in it since the bone continues to flavor the broth after it's been frozen.

Ingredients

- 2 whole tomatoes, split into thirds
- ½ quarts water
- 2 cups navy beans, dried
- 1 ½ pounds large ham with bone
- 1 cup potatoes, peeled and diced
- 1 cup celery, finely sliced
- 1 cup carrots, finely sliced

Directions

1. Bring 1 quart of water to a boil in a saucepan over high heat. Drop one whole tomato into the boiling water, blanch for three minutes, then plunge the tomato into cold water. Replace the first tomato with the second. Peel the tomatoes by running them under cold water.
2. To prepare the tomatoes, split them in half and scrape out the seeds on a clean cutting board. Once the tomatoes have been diced, set them aside.
3. In a large stockpot, bring 2 ½ quarts of water and beans to a boil over high heat. After 2 minutes of boiling, take the beans from the heat and set them aside for 1 hour to cool.
4. Cook for 2 hours, or until the beans are practically

cooked, after which remove the ham bone and discard it.

5. Simmer for another hour after adding the potatoes, celery, carrots, and blanched tomatoes.
6. Using a paring knife, take away the ham bone and chop the flesh before returning it to the beans. Allow to cool to room temperature before serving.

Final Words

I've had my fair share of ups and downs over the last few years. Greetings and farewells are exchanged. There is a difference between life and death. It's a rollercoaster ride of successes, setbacks, and uncertainty. But it was you, my lovely pets, who remained unwavered. I didn't care what was going on around me because there you were, my furry little anchors, right in the middle of everything. Making it possible for me to hold on to anything tangible helps to keep me rooted in reality, whole, and in balance.

It's because of my two wonderful dogs that I made it this far. I hope this book has helped you, not only in feeding your pet, but also with bonding them throughout your recipe journey.

See you in my next book!

Contact me via email at boblouisgillington@gmail.com!

Cover photo by Anna Shvets from Pexels.

References

C. (2020, March 29). *10 delicious and healthy dog food recipes you can make at home.* PetBacker Blog. https://www.petbacker.-com.au/blog/how-to/here-are-10-delicious-and-healthy-dog-food-recipes-you-can-make-at-home

Colley, A. (2021, September 14). *10 Healthy Homemade Dog Food Recipes and Organic Treats.* Money Crashers. https://www.moneycrashers.com/homemade-dog-food-treat-recipes/

Doberman Pinscher Dog Breed Information, Pictures, Characteristics & Facts - Dogtime. (2020, June 18). Dog-Time. https://dogtime.com/dog-breeds/doberman-pinscher#/slide/1

Downs, A. (2021a, April 30). *20 World's Best Toy Dog Breeds.* Top Dog Tips. https://topdogtips.com/best-toy-dog-breeds/

Downs, A. (2021b, August 22). *13 Balanced Homemade Dog Food Recipes*. Top Dog Tips. https://topdogtips.com/balanced-homemade-dog-food-recipes/

Elliott, R. B. D. (2017, December 14). *Can My Dog Eat This? A List of Human Foods Dogs Can and Can't Eat*. Healthline. https://www.healthline.com/nutrition/human-foods-for-dogs#TOC_TITLE_HDR_14

Here Are The 5 Best Guard Dog Breeds. (2020, July 23). Petsmont. https://www.petsmont.com/blogs/pets/here-are-the-5-best-guard-dog-breeds

J. (2021, February 4). *9 Vet Approved Homemade Dog Food Recipes for a Thriving Pup*. Avid Pup. https://www.avidpup.com/homemade-dog-food-recipes-vet-approved/

Kanaka, R. (2017, March 31). *Top 20 healthy homemade dog food recipes your dog will love*. The Dog Bakery. https://www.thedogbakery.com/blogs/news/top-20-healthy-homemade-dog-food-recipes-your-dog-will-love

Millan, C. (2020, December 10). *Top 10 Best Guard Dogs | Find the Best for You*. Cesar's Way. https://www.cesarsway.com/top-10-best-guard-dogs/

People Foods to Avoid Feeding Your Pets. (n.d.). ASPCA. https://www.aspca.org/pet-care/animal-poison-control/people-foods-avoid-feeding-your-pets

Sissons, B. (2019, February 15). *Which people foods are safe for dogs?* Medicalnewstoday. https://www.medicalnewstoday.com/articles/324453#which-human-foods-can-dogs-eat

Smith, L. (2021, May 25). *25 of the Most Decorated Dog Breeds*. Newsweek. https://www.newsweek.com/most-decorated-dog-breeds-1592577

Staff, A. (2021, September 22). *People Foods Dogs Can and Can't Eat*. American Kennel Club. https://www.akc.org/expert-advice/nutrition/human-foods-dogs-can-and-cant-eat/

Printed in Great Britain
by Amazon

78774336R00077